A Sunset Book

S0-AWH-662

CAMERA HAWAII

Lighting Your Home

BY THE EDITORIAL STAFFS OF
SUNSET MAGAZINE AND SUNSET BOOKS

Lane Book Company, Menlo Park, California

PREFACE

The first electric light bulb took shape in the hands of Thomas Alva Edison no awesome time ago. But the man who started it all would be dumbfounded to see the evolution of his brightest offspring.

Change was relatively slow over the first few decades after Edison's discovery. It is not difficult to recall the old frame house of our youth, with its dim fixtures, lack of convenience outlets, and the brittle knob-and-tube wiring that went with them. World War II inspired a rush of new equipment. But it has been in the few years since space and electronics became prime concerns that residential lighting has seen the rush of improvements swell to an avalanche.

Specialized controls aid the homeowner in his use of an almost endless variety of types of light and light fixtures. He can have warm light, cool light, bright light, dim light, large light or small. He can turn the garage light on or off when he is in the garage, in the living room, or after he is snug in bed. He can even turn lights on in Duluth when he is in Peoria without giving the matter a thought.

A homeowner setting out to improve on existing light, or to light a new home, is more apt to be demoralized by the wealth of material than by any lack of it. This book tries to reduce the available information to manageable proportions. It deals with light in general enough to give you an idea of the reasoning behind fixture designs of many kinds. It shows applications of different lighting techniques to common problem situations. And, in the last chapter, it provides specific information on fixtures and fixture design for most of the widely used types. The chapter ignores techniques of wiring. The publishers feel that the whole process of wiring is best left to professionals, an attitude shared by insurance companies, municipal building inspectors, and fire departments.

A note on the photographs. As you will see, many of them are taken in daylight. Films are increasingly sensitive, but they still do not see as well as the human eye in many cases. Night photographs under artificial light too often miss important details. In cases of this type, the photographers borrowed a bit of sunshine.

We gratefully acknowledge the contributions of many firms and agencies to the information gathered here. A list of them is on page 96. You may wish to write to their consumer service departments for specific product information.

ALL RIGHTS RESERVED THROUGHOUT THE WORLD. THIS BOOK, OR PARTS THEREOF, MAY NOT BE REPRODUCED IN ANY FORM WITHOUT PERMISSION OF THE PUBLISHERS. FIRST EDITION SEPTEMBER 1963. COPYRIGHT © 1963 BY LANE BOOK COMPANY, MENLO PARK, CALIFORNIA. LIBRARY OF CONGRESS CATALOG CARD NO. 63-20084. TITLE NO. 131.

CONTENTS

CLYDE CHILDRESS

ONCE OVER...LIGHTLY

A sofa of exemplary design placed in a comfortably warm room should guarantee comfort, but it doesn't unless the light in the room lets you sit at ease.

A dinner prepared with care and served with elegance can be a treasured memory, but it probably will not be unless the light in the room encourages guests to linger at the table.

A kitchen equipped with a multitude of automatic time-savers, and limitless work and storage space should guarantee efficiency, but it doesn't unless the light in the room lets you work without eyestrain.

Light, though it has neither shape nor substance of its own, is an ingredient that can make or break your home as a pleasant place to live.

The twentieth century scientist knows a great part of what may usefully be known about light. His measurements of light from different sources are precise. His knowledge of how light will reflect from different colors and materials is equally precise. For example, one study by illuminating engineers shows that you need more light to darn a mound of black socks than you need to mend an equal number of white ones, if you want to get through the task with a minimum of eyestrain.

But.

What cannot be predicted with any precision at all is your reaction to light. You, as an individual, have to be the judge when it is time to light your home. If you enjoy dimly lighted resturants and the kindly light of the moon, you will probably want to repeat these experiences at home. If you like the brightness of beaches of white sand at noon, your home may serve you best if it can be made light and bright to repeat that visual experience. Light is inseparably the handmaiden of mood. It can also be a part of the interior decoration of your home, because it is the element of nature that lets you see.

So lighting the home is as much a matter of taste as it is of scientific calculation. Even with this important reservation, the scientific studies of light and lighting are of value to anyone about to remodel his home, about to repaint a room, or about to buy a new light fixture. If you know what the lighting expert looks for in the matter of plus and minus values in any lighting scheme, you will have an idea of the effect your ideas will produce when they are installed in your home. Breaking the rules of illuminating by precise measurement is safer if you know what the consequence is to be.

Three problems that need solution if a lighting scheme is to be workable are: The level of illumination in the room as a whole, the level of illumination for specific tasks, and the question of glare. Factors that affect these problems are the number and placement of light sources, their total power, their design, and the colors and textures of walls, ceilings, floors, and furnishings in the room, or in a part of the room.

For a solution to be impeccable in the eyes of the illuminating engineer, all these factors would need to be correlated precisely, and matched to the physical capacity of your eyes. For a solution to be comfortable to you, they need only be observed with some care. Often you can arrive at a comfortable solution intuitively.

REFLECTANCE

When you "see" an object, technically your eye reacts to reflected light of a certain intensity and color. The reflected light is given shape by reflected light from other objects, the green wall behind a mahogany chest for example. When there is no light at all, the object does not exist for your eyes, although it continues to exist and may remind your shins sharply. Two qualities affect the reflectance of light from a surface. One is texture. The other is color.

Texture does not appreciably affect the amount of light reflected by a surface. A highly polished one reflects about the same amount of light as a dull surface of the same color. But it reflects the light in a different way.

Dull matte finishes, such as woven cotton cloth, burlap, or flat paints, diffuse the light they reflect, creating a soft glow. Highly polished surfaces send light bouncing back in roughly the same pattern in which it strikes them. The most intense example of this is sun bouncing off the windshield of a car. The commonest home sources of this type, known as specular reflection, are glass, enamel (as in kitchen appliances), and highly polished furniture.

Color dominates the amount of light reflected. The lighter the color, obviously, the greater the reflection. White reflects 80% or more of the light reaching it. Black reflects 10% or less. The palest pastels range between 70% (beige, lilac) and 80% (yellow, rose). The cool colors, blue and green, are in the 73-75% range in pastel shades. Fully pigmented yellow (mustard) reflects 34%

of the light cast on it. A medium brown reflects 24%. Blue and green reflect 20-29%, depending on the particular shade.

There are some limits on the range of reflectance values of floors, walls and ceilings in the home. They are mainly dictated by good common sense. Lighting experts define them this way: 60-85% for ceilings, 35-60% for walls, and 25-30% for floors. If your ceiling is near 85% on the reflectance scale, the walls and floors should be correspondingly high in their range, or you may encounter difficulty in balancing the amounts of reflected light from two adjoining surfaces.

The intensity of light diminishes rapidly as it travels. A shaded lamp with a 100-watt bulb placed near a wall and the ceiling will make a room seem fairly bright. The farther it is moved toward the center of the room, and the closer it gets to the floor, the less bright the room will seem as a whole. The mathematical formula is: Light diminishes as the square of the distance from source to reflecting surface. (In other words, you get a certain amount of light from a source one foot from a surface. You get one-fourth as much if the source is two feet away, one-ninth as much if it is three feet away, and one-sixteenth as much if it is four feet away.)

GLARE

Contrasting light (or color) values form one of the prime tools of good decorating. Without them, as in a room with beige walls, beige rug, and beige furniture, all evenly lighted by a luminous ceiling, the interior would be as interesting as the inside of a pasteboard box. But there can be too much contrast. The human eye can accommodate only a limited range of light intensity without straining. Excessive contrasts in light value are the source of glare.

The obvious kinds of glare are direct and specular. It is easy to discover when an exposed light source is too bright for its surroundings, or when you are confronted by a harsh reflection from window glass. The type most troublesome to correct is reflected or diffused light that is not so obviously out of balance with its surroundings.

Of the dozens of potential glare sources in the modern home, many are the result of conflicts in purposes between two or more elements of the lighting and decorating schemes. A strongly lighted luminous panel in a dark-hued wall might be one example. A light-transmitting lamp shade against a dark wall is another. A third frequent cause is using a light that is ideal for a specific purpose in a way that shines directly in the eyes of someone in another part of the house. In the open-plan house, the problem is often present, and often hard to cure. An example is a light over the dining table that beams over a partition into the eyes of someone sitting on the living room sofa.

But most glare problems are the products of lighting for work. Examples of this are strong light for reading, with the white pages of the book set against the too-dark background of a desk top; strong light on a kitchen counter but deep shadows under overhanging cabinets, and light so strongly directional that it distorts the appearance of a three-dimensional object with many surface planes by creating deep shadows near highlights (a number of crafts and hobbies may include projects that fit in this category).

The solutions for glare problems are plentiful. Many times one may be solved by moving a light source a bit farther from a light wall, or closer to a dark one. Reducing the wattage of a bulb in a portable lamp may sometimes help. Replacing the shade on a lamp with one that is closer in light value to the surroundings may solve a glare problem. Larger shades can hide a light bulb that would produce a hot spot on a smaller shade, or that could be seen directly by someone standing nearby. If none of these recourses look promising, you may need different fixtures, more fixtures, or a new coat of paint or paper on an offending wall.

LEVELS OF LIGHTING

Houses have rooms because a house must shelter a wide range of activities, ranging from public ones such as entertaining guests to private ones such as dressing. It follows that each of these activities should be lighted to suit the mood associated with it, and to make the performance of specific tasks as efficient as possible.

Lighting experts, through their research programs, have established general standards for lighting each room. The figures are based on typical uses of the rooms in average American homes. Their findings are usually expressed in mathematical measurements of foot-candles (the amount of light generated by one plumber's candle, measured one foot from the flame), or lumens (an arbitrary unit of light intensity). These need translating to be of use in the home.

The following table is a simplified version of these measurements. If you use the index numbers as a guide to the maximum number of incandescent watts you can obtain from your electric system, you will be able to achieve the experts' recommended effects without difficulty. Note that you will not necessarily use all of this wattage at any one time. Also, fluorescent tubes produce three to four times as much light per watt as incandescents, a factor you will need to consider if you use both types, or all fluorescent light.

	Watts per sq. ft.
Kitchen	10
Living room	10
Bedroom	8½
Laundry	8½
Work benches	8½
Bathroom	8
Dining room	5½
Hallways	5½

These figures take into account only potential amounts of light; useful results come only with well-designed fixtures. Nor do they take into account reflectance factors, which vary with colors in a decorating scheme and with types of architecture. You may argue that the living room should not be as brightly lit as the kitchen, and you will be right. But you will be right because the decor in living rooms is usually darker than that in kitchens, and because lighting fixtures used in living rooms produce a more diffused light than the utilitarian fixtures in kitchens, where the cook must see to do the smallest of tasks. The result is that you probably would need more watts of light power in the living room to make it as bright as the kitchen. The architecture of the house makes a considerable difference, too. A wood-paneled, open-plan house may need close to the maximum listed in the table of watts to be bright, while a conventional house with four full walls and light-colored ceilings in every room might be adequately lighted by a third as many watts.

TYPES OF LIGHTING

Another of the reasons for the table of watts not being an exact thing is that artificial light sources are of several types. They can be direct or indirect, diffused or spot, structural or portable, or general or task. These distinctions are not absolute ones, but they are useful because they help to show how much light you may expect from different types of fixtures. The reasons for the distinctions are best stated by defining them.

Direct. Any light that goes straight from the source to the object you wish to light is direct. Spotlights used for decorative light are the most obvious example. Most work lights in kitchens or shops are also direct. Any floor or table lamp, and most ceiling-mounted fixtures have some direct lighting qualities.

Indirect. When the source is hidden from view, and all the light visible to you is reflected from walls or the ceiling, the light is purely indirect. Examples are cove lighting, in which light is bounced off the upper walls and ceiling, and cornice or valance lighting, in which it washes a wall from a concealed source. Floor and table lamps which send light up from the open top of a shade are partially indirect.

Spot. The light is channeled by reflecting surfaces, usually a silver coating inside the bulb, so that most of it is concentrated in a small area, even at considerable distances from the source. The main use is decorative if indoors. Outdoors, PAR-type spotlights find frequent use in lighting patios.

Diffused. A matter of degree more than the other distinctions made here, diffusion simply means that the light is passed through a material that spreads it over a larger area than the source itself. An inside-frosted light bulb diffuses the light made by the filament. Fluorescent light is automatically diffused by the tube-coating that makes it visible. Shades that transmit some light diffuse the light from a bulb. Plastic panels in luminous ceilings are perhaps the extreme example. In general, the more diffused light is, the easier it is to view regardless of intensity, because more of the field of vision is occupied by a light area.

Structural. As the name indicates, structural light units are those which are incorporated into the architecture of the house. They are integral to the house rather than to a temporary decorative scheme within it. Examples of structural lighting are recessed ceiling units, ceiling panels, luminous ceilings, coves, valances and cornices.

Portable and Mounted fixtures. The broad term covers floor and table lamps, and ceiling and wall-mounted lamps which have some decorative purpose of their own, or which are entirely utilitarian, such as a mechanic's trouble light. Most of them can be removed or replaced without disturbing any other aspect of the room.

General light. In effect the sum of all the light generated in a room, its purposes are to aid navigation and to reveal the room as a whole. The basis of most general lighting schemes is the overhead source, whether it is ceiling-attached or one of the structural types. Sunlight comes from overhead, so the most natural seeming light comes from overhead sources. All general lighting aids in the performance of tasks by supplementing the local source of light and providing background illumination for the task.

Task Light. Also called local light, it is most often a floor or table lamp—or a mounted fixture that gives the same effect—in the public or social parts of a house. In the working areas, it is the light source closest to the work you are doing. It is frequently less diffused than general light, but not always. Luminous ceilings provide excellent all-purpose lighting in kitchens and baths. Local lighting also has a secondary function. Each local light source augments the general level of illumination.

These categories repeatedly overlap. But they are still a help if you work out lighting with each of them in mind. As you look at that dark and unusable corner, do you think it needs more general light, or should it have local light so you can read there? Should it be direct to light a house plant, or diffused? Does the corner lend itself to a structural installation like a ceiling panel, or will a floor lamp create interest along a barren stretch of wall? How will one type or another fit in with the color and texture of the wall? How bright should it be to serve its purpose?

The designers of the lighting schemes on the next 70 pages asked themselves questions like these. The solutions are good ones in the technical sense. With substitutions of design to match decor in your house, they may be right for you.

Lighting THE INTERIOR

THE ENTRY AREA

The entry hall is a guest's first impression of the interior of your home. It is also a bridge between you and callers.

Ideally, an entry hall is spacious, but clearly separate from the living areas of the house. In a large home, the entry area can be a room defined by walls and doorways. In a smaller home, good lighting together with screening devices can often help replace walls by directing and limiting the view of callers without necessarily blinding them.

A basic problem of entry hall lighting is to achieve a level of illumination that makes coming indoors or going out easy for the eyes. Light on the porch should be roughly balanced by that inside the door. To avoid glare in the face of either host or caller, fixtures overhead or high on the wall are often the simplest solution. Well diffused eye-level light may be equally effective. Any change of floor level, however slight, should be clearly visible, which in most cases means the fixture should cast light down in a fairly wide pool. (For the outside elements of entry lighting, see pages 64-66.)

In addition to such functional light, to let you and your guests see each other, entry hall light is largely decorative. It is decorative for two reasons, the first to introduce guests to your home, and the second to focus the attention of unexpected callers in a limited space. Often this means focusing the light on one wall, on which some object of interest is located. Or it may mean a decorative fixture that creates a pool of light as a focus. Some of the photographs in the decora-

DEARBORN-MASSAR

Lighted display case makes focal point in entryway. Fluorescent tube concealed behind facer at top of cabinet provides light for flower arrangements, paintings, which can be changed easily for new interest. Switch located on wall of case at left side.

tive light section (pages 20-25) are of entry hall arrangements.

If a wall faces the doorway, the ceiling-recessed eyeball unit is one choice for lighting something on that wall. Cone or bullet fixtures are another. They can be used singly for highlight effects, or in series for a more even wash of light. Wash light can also be obtained from troffer, cornice, or wall-bracket assemblies, using fluorescent or lumiline tubes or series of bulbs.

If the light must go at one side in an open area, a dramatic display can be lighted by ceiling units that consume little space. To limit the view, it works best on the latch side of the door.

Often you can save the expense of added wiring and fixtures by installing glass or plastic wall panels that pick up light from adjoining rooms.

MORLEY BAER

The ceiling troffer provides light on floor of entry. Display table is lighted by small spotlight (behind door, at left). Other light on panel at right.

ERNEST BRAUN

DEARBORN-MASSAR

A diffusing globe mounted on ceiling is augmented by a wire-glass skylight. The garden beyond glass wall is also lighted at night for interest.

Wall at one side of entryway blocks view into living room. Soffit lighting floods bench for visitors, a floral arrangement and painting. Hall leads to bedrooms.

RICHARD FISH

Diffusing globe above doorway provides general light, also creates shadow pattern on outside of diffusing glass panel for decorative interest.

ERNEST BRAUN

Open bottom of diffusing cylinder allows strong light to reach floor in entryway. Table with flower arrangement is at edge of the field of light, draws attention.

MAYNARD L. PARKER

Slender fixture in ceiling creates pool of bright light just inside doorway without being bright in eyes of arriving guests. Windows let light out.

RICHARD FISH

Two recessed units with frosted glass diffusing panels light this hallway. Sliding screen (a shortened folding door) can block view of room.

ROGER STURTEVANT

JULIUS SHULMAN

RICHARD FISH

Pin-hole spotlight above statue lights just enough of entry area to make it safe. Stairway to main living area is lighted from the upper level.

Spotlight in bullet fixture (at left in photo) reflects from ceiling. Other spots are in entry garden on other side of living room wall, and under carport.

Like the photo above, this entry uses indirect light to achieve a soft atmosphere. Lamps are recessed in ceiling above planter to reflect off leaves, wall.

BRIGHT
CONVERSATION CORNERS

In a harshly lighted room, full of glare and shadows, the most blameless of men sit tensely, as if awaiting the arrival of a suspicious lieutenant of police. It is difficult to feel at ease if you cannot see the reactions of the person to whom you speak, and sense at the same time that you are plainly visible to him.

Good light for conversation should be diffuse, and flexible to fit the several moods you may wish to achieve. By diffuse, lighting experts mean that no light should be used so that a person moving in established foot-traffic patterns, or looking about the room, can see an exposed bulb or other harsh light directly. This kind of diffusion can be obtained by indirect lighting schemes, by well-designed lamp shades, by spotlights aimed away from chairs or other furniture rather than at them, or by diffusing panels. Different levels of illumination can be obtained by

HUGH N. STRATFORD

In open, high-ceilinged home, row of direct-indirect fixtures (one bulb shines up, another down) lights wall at right. Bullet lamps under eaves light garden outside uncurtained window wall, keep glass from being black, or reflecting interior. Table lamp, ceiling fixture provide local light for reading, dining.

using three-effect portable or fixed lamps, by using a dimmer system, or just by having more lights to turn on or off.

The spaciousness of the open-plan home creates some special problems of lighting. The traditional ceiling-fixture-plus-portable-lamps lighting scheme, still deservedly popular in living rooms of conventional design, often is inadequate to the task. Glass walls and high ceilings usually do not offer enough reflective surface. Architects and designers have developed several attractive solutions, most of which involve lighting large areas of the ceiling, or washing an entire wall with light. Known generally as "broad source lighting," approaches of this type work on the thesis that a relatively large amount of light can be spread evenly over a large area to provide comfortable illumination. The sources often are visible, but are of low-brightness levels so they can be viewed comfortably, much like a window in the daytime.

Some of these broad-source lighting techniques, especially the luminous ceiling, diminish the need for standard floor or table lamps, except for reading. However, they also eliminate shadows and volumes, tending to make a space uninteresting. Lamps afford the opposite, a definition of the volumes in a room, and therefor a sense of variety.

There are literally thousands of lamp designs intended for use in conversation areas, varied to match every conceivable type of decor. The photographs in this (and other) sections are chosen to show basic arrangements of lighting, not to demonstrate specific fixture designs.

The general recommendations are that there always be at least two sources of light in a room area, to avoid deep shadows and to keep all shadows from falling in the same direction. If all lamps are incandescent, the minimum amount of safe light for getting around and for conversation can be obtained from as few as three watts per square foot in a light-colored room, or five watts in a darker one. Fluorescent tubes generate about three times as much light per watt as do incandescent lamps.

Fluorescent tubes in coves on side walls provide general illumination. Their light is augmented by table lamps that provide highlights, local light.

Table lamps frame fireplace, set visual limits for conversation area. Glass half of high interior wall lets light spread from one room to another.

LELAND LEE

CLYDE CHILDRESS

Combination cove-and-soffit designed by Goodwin Steinberg provides local light through plastic panels in cove bottom. Unit dimmer-controlled.

ERNEST BRAUN

DOUGLAS SIMMONDS

Window seat is lighted by a combination cove-and-soffit dropped well down from ceiling to lend to feeling of cozy shelter. Design by Mario Corbett.

Soffit (shown in pure form, enclosed in section of dropped ceiling so all light is directed down) is classic way to light sofa. Design by Fred Earl Norris.

ERNEST BRAUN

DARROW WATT

Valances (above) on adjoining walls provide all light in conversation area. Table lamps elsewhere.

Cove-and-soffit lights sofa, book bindings in the large library. Unit uses incandescent bulbs spaced widely.

DEARBORN-MASSAR

DARROW WATT

Outdoor low-voltage lights housed in dropped section of ceiling make overlapping pools of light on sofa. Transformer, switch hidden behind.

A dropped section of ceiling, supported by long center beam, holds three recessed "high-hat" fixtures near its front edge to light sofa, two "eye-ball" fixtures near wall to back-light a long planter.

ERNEST BRAUN

Rows of incandescent bulbs along edges of shoji-like ceiling panels provide soft glow in living room. John Matthias design. Construction details on page 87.

Row of suspended fixtures makes visual limit for conversation area, marks out limits of hallway behind the arm chairs. Design is by Richard Banta.

PRESCOLITE

Recessed units provide general illumination for conversation. Suspended glass shapes make decorative focus points, use low-wattage bulbs to avoid glare.

RICHARD FISH

ARTCREST

Translucent panels, opaque acousti-
cal tile combined in luminous ceiling
assembly to light small area of room;
decorative panels in center are main
light unit; single panel near door.

DEARBORN-MASSAR

Plastic panels behind sofa transmit light from entry.
Soft glow augmented by well-diffused lamp suspended
on poles from high ceiling. Design by Terry & Moore.

ARTCREST

Luminous ceiling panels and luminous wall are com-
bined. Fluorescent tubes mounted in ceiling send light
down V-shaped panel set in wall to produce a soft glow.

DECORATIVE TOUCHES

Decorative light, an almost limitless subject, is light which draws attention to an object, to a group of objects, or to itself.

Almost anything you own can be a candidate: Draperies, master pieces of cabinetry, fireplaces, paintings, or plants. By means of a well-designed fixture, use of light itself can be a means of decorating, as some of the photographs show.

Rules are few. As a starting point, you may find it wise to decide how permanent your interest is in a certain object, or in having certain places as display areas. It is not always easy to revise a lighting scheme after it is installed. In the same vein, spotlights can be tricky to work with. Some experimenting with lights on extension cords can tell you where to make the permanent installation that will serve your purpose. Some built-in choices of effect can help to keep decorative light fresh and interesting. Multiple switches can permit you to control spotlight effects by using two, four, or six at a time. Colored light bulbs or tinted covers give you still more freedom to alter decorative effects with

ERNEST BRAUN

Fireplaces are frequent choice for decorative lighting schemes. This tile-faced custom design by John Kapel is bathed in the glow of two semi-recessed eye ball units, which can be aimed for effect. The one at the right is directed toward the carved figure and is turned on to show spread of light (the other is off).

the seasons or for parties. Dimmer systems offer yet another effective control.

The increasing emphasis on day-lighting in contemporary architecture developed a new field of decorative light, the combination skylight and ceiling troffer or luminous panel. Units of this type allow day and night display of the same object in similar light. Modern furniture finishes and textile dyes do not fade in the sun as fast as antique pieces might. Diffusing materials are available that block infra-red light. Antiques can be safely exposed beneath them. Book bindings are another material which should be guarded against too much direct sun. Plant materials, on the other hand, benefit from unfiltered sunlight (though they must have effective ventilation to keep the air around them moist and not too hot).

Oil paintings are subject to deterioration under direct sunlight, but benefit from being exposed to day and night lighting. A wide variety of inexpensive fixtures much like those used in museums are available for lighting framed pictures. The fixture should cast even light over the entire framed area to retain the artist's intended effect. Recessed ceiling spotlights with lens can be installed to light a precise area.

ERNEST BRAUN

Clear bulbs behind louvers in the recessed ceiling units produce the striped effect on draperies. Exposed miniature bulbs are in chandelier over table.

JULIUS SHULMAN

Standard incandescent bulbs mounted in recesses in the ceiling light a book wall. Openings are covered with frosted glass (see page 84 for detail).

ROGER STURTEVANT

Adjustable bullet lamps mounted to shine on two walls provide flexible light. Note that some are aimed parallel to ceiling for reflection, others for highlights.

Decorative 21

DARROW WATT

Honeycomb louvers in these soffits spread light out to illuminate both the book wall and the floor. A second row on the other side of wall balances these.

Two exposed bulbs shine up to reflect off a white ceiling, and down through a plastic diffuser to display shelf in dining room. Design by Henrik Bull.

MORLEY BAER

Troffer-skylight combination gives around the clock attention to antique Chinese chest in dining room. Diffusers filter infra-red rays. Campbell & Wong.

GLENN CHRISTIANSEN

CHAS. R. PEARSON

DARROW WATT

Indoor garden is dramatically lit by corrugated glass skylight in daylight hours. At night, sparkles of light from perforated cylinder in hall, spotlight mounted on beam brighten it. Design is by Earl Lehr Powell.

In corner, slit window provides light by day, a troffer takes over at night to avoid a dark, gloomy spot in room.

GEORGE DE GENNARO

PHOTO-ART

Four spots over 60-inch square panel light tinted photo printed on translucent paper, mounted on glass sheet.

Skylight, luminous ceiling combined to call attention to Japanese print, flower arrangement. Mosher & Drew.

ERNEST BRAUN

ERNEST BRAUN

MARTHA ROSMAN

Above, shelf over pass-through lighted by fluorescent tubes. Structure is like wall bracket. See page 82. Plastic diffuser is on top only.

Above left, rows of tubes recessed in top, bottom of book case call attention to it, display shelf below. They also light hallway behind.

Five tube lights make highlights on this book and storage wall. One is behind facer above painting. Two others below painting, two vertical strips (behind shields) at each end.

CHAS. R. PEARSON

DARROW WATT

R. WENKAM

TOM BURNS JR.

Fixtures can be used to make patterns of light on a bare wall. Top, bottom fixtures are manufactured. Center, ¼x2 strips of wood set in ring around bulb.

A cluster of perforated cylinders cast sparkling play of light onto cork wall. Downlight highlights sculpture. Plastic panels lighted from other room.

LIGHT TO DINE BY

From the great hall of the medieval castle until the appearance of electric light, the dining table was usually lighted by candles. In the reign of King Arthur, the light source for a palatial board was a huge candleholder, the original chandelier. Candles were placed on smaller tables. Now there are many ways to approximate the same effects. And the candle still is a cheerful choice.

The purpose of the central light in a dining room is to illuminate the table and its pleasurable burden of food and to cast a soft, flattering light on the guests gathered around.

Intimate dining and subdued light are forever linked. Formal dining and decorative light are equally inseparable. Family dinners usually take place in bright, cheerful light. Lighting for the

RICHARD FISH

Bulbs in each of three diffusing cylinders of glass cast a strong light down onto the table top while allowing a softer light to escape and reflect from walls and draperies near table in formal dining room. Design, Holmes & Sellery.

merely useful, such as setting and clearing the table is another factor to consider in designing the lighting system for dining.

The dining table in many modern homes serves for intimate, formal and family dining by turns. The several purposes require a system of some versatility. Many designers achieve it with a three-effect or dimmer-controlled central light, and one or more separately controlled supplementary light sources.

Intimate dining, as the word suggests, means the focus of attention is on the diners. The simplest means of obtaining a properly subdued atmosphere is a candle. Next simplest is a single overhead unit not powerful enough to cause more than a faint glow on surrounding walls. Dark-hued surroundings make the task easier than do brighter colors because reflected light is less.

For formal dining, the elegance of the room is a factor that often can be edited by lighting to emphasize the table, centerpiece, china, and silver. Many well-designed ceiling fixtures contain a down-light which can be controlled separately from the general lights. Ones that do not can be supplemented by ceiling-recessed fixtures to call attention to the table. Valance, cornice, or other techniques can serve to highlight a decorated wall, but generally should not dominate.

To avoid glare in the eyes of diners, ceiling attached fixtures should be centered above the table, with the lowest part 36 inches above it. Recessed lights or luminous panels should be about equal to the table in size for the same reason, and to avoid deep shadow.

Reel-type fixture allows hosts to control brightness of table (above). The closer the large diffusing globe is to the table, the brighter it becomes.

Reel-equipped traditional chandelier form lights the table. A cove running the length of the room provides general illumination. Design by C. B. Alford.

CHAS. R. PEARSON

PRESCOLITE

ART HUPY

R. WENKAM

A cluster of low-wattage bulbs seems less bright when viewed directly, but gives as much light as a large bulb.

At left, diffusing plastic shades table light. Cone open at bottom for highlights. Shoji panels close off kitchen, transmit pleasant light from it.

CAMERA HAWAII

Elongated Japanese paper lantern and candles provide the illumination for a formal dining table. The lantern uses low-wattage bulbs to avoid hot spots and glare. Recessed spotlights brighten the plastic panel-enclosed garden at night. Panels also admit daylight to room, which faces on busy street.

DARROW WATT

Two fluorescent tubes light panel above table. Kitchen lights glow through plastic panel set in wall.

TOM BURNS JR.

Combination skylights-luminous panels provide day, night illumination in dining room and kitchen (behind divider). Sources hidden from diners by beam. Ceiling fixture over table (at left) provides the local light.

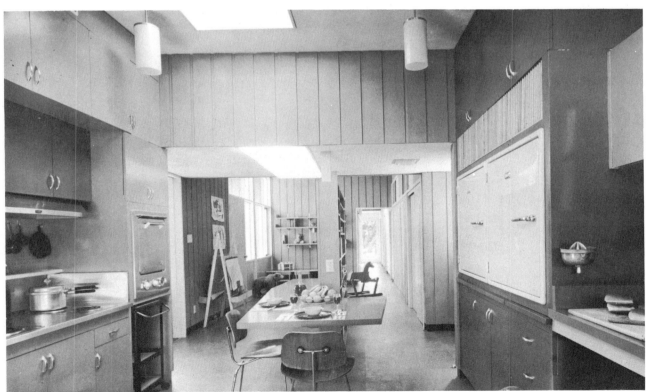

ERNEST BRAUN

A manufactured ceiling panel lighted by fluorescent tubes illuminates family dining table. Panel about equals table top in size for even light. Hooded ceil-ing fixtures over kitchen work counter, semi-recessed fixtures in hallway can boost illumination level if on, or enhance intimacy if left off.

HALLWAYS AND STAIRS

Technically, there is no great difference between the way you light an elegant entry stair and the way you light a rough, utilitarian basement stair. For maximum foot safety, each landing and at least the first few steps leading away from it should be lighted clearly. If the treads are of uniform size, persons using the stairs can climb or descend confidently once they have gotten into the rhythm of stepping up or down.

Stairway light that shines in your eyes can cause confusion, especially in otherwise dimly lighted surroundings, and perhaps cause a misstep. This is especially important if a light is suspended over the center of the stair case so that it can be seen from both the top and bottom landings of the flight. The source should not be directly visible from the top. A harsh light inside the shade should not be visible from below. A diffusing shade, such as the Japanese globe, works best if it is sized to the bulb it contains so as to diffuse light evenly. If the diffusing shade itself is rather bright, it should be placed close enough to a wall to brighten the wall. Otherwise it may stand out as a glare against a dark background. Shades which transmit very little light through their sides should be large enough to cast an even pool of light over an entire landing and several steps. The height at which they are mounted also controls the spread of light. If light from other rooms does not clearly illuminate a landing not reached by the stairway fix-

MORLEY BAER

Central hallway is lighted day and night by combination skylight and luminous ceiling. Spotlights are mounted well above plastic diffusing panels on 4-foot module that provides fairly even effect at night. PAR-type bulbs, 75- or 150-watt, are especially suited to use if skylights are not insulating type in cold country.

ture, a wall-mounted direct-indirect lamp may be advisable.

For maximum safety, night lights at top and bottom will warn the unwary who must approach the stairway in darkness.

Any stairway light should have a three-way switch or some other device that permits control from either level.

Hall lighting is simpler. Ceiling-attached fixtures are the commonest solution. In single story homes with flat roofs, the combination skylight-troffer or skylight-luminous panel provides an excellent solution for interior halls that get little or no daylight otherwise. Light should be directed carefully to avoid glare in a long hall. For efficiency, lamps can be located to illuminate doors or storage space. In general, use one fixture for each 10 linear feet of hallway.

DEARBORN-MASSAR

Strips of light across a long interior hall are from skylights. Device can be adapted to use with fluorescent tubes in homes without skylights.

CLYDE CHILDRESS

In home with attic crawl space, skylights and luminous ceiling panels combine for day, night light. A single 150-watt floodlight is 2 feet above each panel.

DARROW WATT

An out-dated fixture can be replaced by a shielded fluorescent tube without changing wiring. Shield should be 6 inches from ceiling to spread light.

GLENN CHRISTIANSEN

Plastic diffusing panels mounted in the bottoms of opaque boxes direct major part of light down to hall floor. Vents at top brighten ceiling.

DARROW WATT

Troughs of light are mounted 7 feet off the floor to minimize sense of height in a hallway with 9-foot ceilings. Colored glass in cut-out holes on sides.

ERNEST BRAUN

Interior hallway gets feeling of daylight from luminous ceiling using fluorescent tubes behind plastic panels. Design by H. Douglas Byles.

ERNEST BRAUN

Simple custom-made unit consists of 1x12 finished to match ceiling, with bamboo trivets set in beneath 60-watt bulbs recessed into ceiling.

DARROW WATT

Stairway light uses custom-built shade to avoid glare. Glass panes in octagonal frame covered by fragments of colored glass glued to them.

MORLEY BAER

DEARBORN-MASSAR

Stairwell is lighted by a large hanging fixture identical to the one in foreground. Metal shields direct light to sides. Unit is open at bottom.

Deep shade on stairwell fixture keeps glare from eyes of persons ascending stairs. Shade diffuses light well, brightens wall behind the fixture.

IN THE BATH

A poorly lighted bathroom mirror likely as not is responsible for the man who sets out into the world weekday mornings with patches of stubble beneath his lip and along his jaw line. The same deficient lighting arrangement can cause a woman to arrive downtown with lipstick and rouge mis-matched.

Bath and dressing rooms with good lighting are the beginning of good grooming.

Light for shaving, or for makeup, should fall on the face of the person using a mirror, rather than on the mirror itself. Light directed at the mirror will be reflected just as faithfully as a human image, which is to say that it will produce more glare than useful light. But a well-lighted face will be reflected for what it is.

Experts recommend that three lights be used with a bath or dressing table mirror, one of them above, and two others at eye level and spaced at least 30 inches apart on centers. Incandescent bulbs of 60 watts are suitable for each fixture. Fluorescent tubes of 20 watts, 24 inches long, can be used at the sides of the mirror; tubes

A unit at each side of the mirror augments luminous ceiling to avoid shadows under jaw, lip or nose. Sources should be shielded by plastic or other diffusing material. Idea can be used with any overhead light.

above the mirror should equal the width of that part of the mirror above the lavatory.

This is by no means the only solution. The main point is that the light fall in a way that avoids shadows, especially under the jaw line. Incandescent light most often should be shielded by plastic or a heavily frosted (flashed opal) glass, although an effective form of mirror lighting is the theater type, consisting of a row of low-wattage bare bulbs across the top and down two sides.

If you use fluorescent tubes, the Deluxe warm white types give the best rendition of flesh tones for makeup.

In a small bath, the mirror lights may provide enough illumination for all purposes. Compartmented baths require at least one light in each compartment. Ordinary fixtures are suitable in all areas but the shower stall, where vapor-proof ceiling fixtures are both necessary and more efficient. Switches for shower lights are safer if they are some distance from the stall itself.

A night light is a good idea, especially in children's baths.

Luminous ceilings are suitable for use in baths. Special care should be taken to avoid spaces that would allow moisture to collect above them.

DARROW WATT

Four rows of fluorescent tubes are used in this soffit, over a wide countertop and lavatory. A second soffit over the shower reflects in the mirror.

DOUGLAS SIMMONDS

Small fluorescent tubes concealed beneath plastic top in dressing table to augment light from unit in ceiling above mirror. See photo, page 38.

ERNEST BRAUN

Woman's dressing table is lighted much like one in photo above. Two rows of tubes are adequate for narrower surface; vertical light at sides could help.

R. WENKAM

Honeycomb louvers allow twice as much light as a solid diffuser, but should not be used near shower because they allow moisture to seep into fixture.

ERNEST BRAUN

A combination skylight and luminous ceiling makes bath bright, shadow-free for shaving, makeup. Unit designed by Henry Hill uses incandescent light.

R. WENKAM

Separate lavatory, makeup table each lighted by two fluorescent tubes placed vertically at sides of mirrors to minimize face shadows. Design, Frank Slavsky.

MAYNARD L. PARKER

A row of closely spaced small-wattage bulbs across the top of a mirror serves same purpose as long tube fixture. Design is by Kipp Stewart.

MAYNARD L. PARKER

GEORGE DE GENNARO

Recommended formula (extreme left) has ceiling light, vertical light at each side of mirror in small bath. All units have fluorescent tubes.

Hinged wings on mirror can be used to reflect light onto face from the luminous ceiling above. Dressing table design is by Mosher & Drew.

ERNEST BRAUN

DOUGLAS SIMMONDS

ERNEST BRAUN

Enclosed shower stalls require special vapor-proof lighting fixtures, of the type mounted on wall.

Another type, recessed in ceiling, is also suitable for showers. It is best to locate switch at a distance.

Tub baths do not create as much water vapor in air, but lights directly above should be vapor-proof.

MASTER SUITES

After the wearying grind of a business day, most men would like a quiet corner at home, where they can relax in uninterrupted quiet. Women, too, enjoy a calm interlude between the end of the housekeeping day and bedtime.

Typically, today's home affords parents complete privacy from the outer world only in the master bedroom. Such a sheltered nook should be a cozy place with comfortable furniture where adults can watch television, read, or just sit and talk. The general lighting in an area intended for this kind of relaxation should be soft, to preserve the mood of intimacy that makes a retreat just that, but supplemented for such seeing tasks as reading or sewing.

In a room with lounge chairs, a bed, or a sprawling Hawaiian hikiee, ceiling fixtures will be a source of glare to reclining persons whose gaze falls upon the ceiling as easily as it does upon the walls, unless the light source is well diffused and not too much brighter than the ceiling. Ceiling-recessed fixtures, or ceiling-attached fixtures tend to be less distracting than chande-

DOUGLAS SIMMONDS

Three recessed ceiling units of a manufactured type are concealed behind a beam above headboard of this bed. The units can be controlled separately so night reading will not cause glare in eyes of person wishing to sleep. A small vanity table to right of the bed contains a special light. See the photo on page 35.

lier types, except for hanging fixtures that direct most of their light upward. A dimmer can be very useful in adjusting ceiling light to a comfortable intensity.

For television watching, the wall behind the set should be lighted to minimize contrast between the screen and its background. The background light should not appear as bright as the screen, or it may distract your eye. Valances, wall brackets, and ceiling recessed units (combined with skylights, if day-lighting of the wall is an advantage to you) are all useful for the purpose. Small portable lamps with shades that transmit only a small amount of light can be placed at either or both sides of the set. If the television set is placed diagonally in a corner, a small lamp can be put behind it. A ceiling fixture alone will light a small room. Care should be taken to avoid having any source of light reflect in the picture tube.

For reading in bed, the general techniques for any reading corner apply (see page 46). Light should be diffused to avoid glare on the pages. Hooded lamps are not recommended, because they do not let light escape upward from the lamp to reflect from walls and ceiling, and because they cast too constricted a pool of light to avoid a sense of glare.

R. WENKAM

ROGER STURTEVANT

A large soffit provides general illumination for master suite and its large, comfortable sofa. Two rows of fluorescent tubes are behind plastic panels.

STEVEN C. WILSON

A troffer located at the intersection of wall and ceiling provides general illumination. Ceiling-suspended fixture is mainly decorative.

A variation on the Hawaiian hikiee (left) is retreat for reading. Fluorescent tube plus incandescent light are hidden in cavity in corner for light.

JULIUS SHULMAN

The reel-lamp at this bedside can be raised or lowered to achieve desired illumination level. Lamp has a plastic diffusing disc across its face to diffuse light *for reading. Light-colored wood wall behind bed is good reflecting agent. For bed reading, lamp should be slightly above eye level, about 16 inches to side.*

DEARBORN-MASSAR

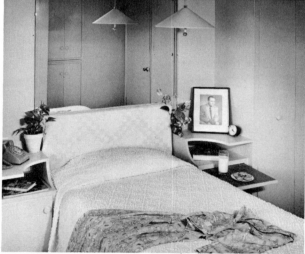

FRANK L. GAYNOR

A reel-lamp similar to one above also provides light for person using mirror. Note that diffusing disc cannot be seen with lamp at eye level; avoids glare.

Fiberglass panels (left) allow soft glow of light to brighten bedroom wall. A row of fluorescent tubes inside closet is source. Note ceiling lights.

DARROW WATT

Large, lightweight plastic diffuser spreads soft, even light over room. Dimmer control adds to flexibility.

R. WENKAM

Sprawling Hawaiian hikiee provides an ideal place to relax, nap, or read. The table lamps at either side are equipped with diffusing bowls to permit reading without eyestrain. Background is light-colored.

ERNEST BRAUN

Cheerful, dancing light from a fireplace makes this bedroom corner cozy. Simple floor lamp offers adequate illumination for reading, light sewing. General light in ceiling.

PLAY AREAS
FOR CHILDREN

Children's rooms are a special case for two reasons. One is that a child develops rapidly in both size and interests, meaning that lighting demands can change just as rapidly over the span of a very few years. Second, the child does a great deal of "living" in the sanctum of his or her room, which is living and bedroom and hobby shop to its young tenant. Children from their first walking year through late teens deserve comfortable privacy from the intrusions of adults (just as adults need refuge from the intrusions of their offspring).

Toddlers and pre-schoolers spend much of their time wallowing about the floor. Even if they have tables, size keeps them close to the ground, so lighting should be designed to make the floor a useful work surface. The flooring serves best if it is light in color, and not too highly polished. Ceiling-attached or recessed fixtures large enough to cast fairly even light over open floor space are safe and practical. Portable

ERNEST BRAUN

A ceiling of plate glass provides daylight for this playroom. After dark, a series of manufactured units recessed in ceiling (above windows at extreme left, in main ceiling at right) provide even light across entire floor through frosted glass diffusing plates. Hood lamp illuminates the fish tank on wall.

lamps are not always advisable because they fall over too easily, and because convenience outlets are too intriguing to curious infants or toddlers. Existing outlets can be covered with blank face plates for a room that becomes a nursery. If you install convenience outlets high off the floor in a nursery, they might be located so they can later be converted to use for wall-brackets or other lighting units.

With school age, the desk becomes central to the lighting scheme. With it, boys usually want a handy display case for souvenirs of assorted triumphs, and girls want a vanity table for the first tentative stabs at make-up. Typically, a boy's room will have the standard ceiling fixture, and either two table lamps or the businesslike fluorescent work light. A girl's room, where the desk also serves as a vanity table, often is lighted the same way, except that the table lamps may need to be suited for use both with a mirror and homework. In either case, the arrangements can be compatible with desk lighting requirements (see pages 46 to 49) without sacrificing the essentials of design that make them acceptable to their users.

If a youngster cultivates a specialized hobby, he may need more elaborate lighting. See the chapter on hobbies and work shops, pages 56-62.

GERALD RATTO

A row of semi-recessed ceiling units along ridge of sloped ceiling lights floor. Units are about a foot square; most of them use 150-watt bulbs.

ERNEST BRAUN

This family and play room uses solution much like one in photo above, a series of semi-recessed ceiling units over main work and play areas. Design, Henrik Bull.

Left, Japanese globe suspended well above floor is good choice for playroom if it is sturdy enough to stand occasional buffetings from thrown objects.

CHAS. R. PEARSON

Children's rooms   43

Multi-purpose work bench for three boys has light for each. Hooded lamps are high enough to avoid glare. Light sources in ceiling aid general level of illumination in room.

TOM BURNS JR.

TOM BURNS JR

In same playroom, table is lighted by reel-lamp with plastic diffusing disc in shade. Fixtures of this type are ideal for any table games.

ROBERT COX

Sisters share this desk and display case. Plastic hoods on lamps allow light to spread properly; opaque hoods are not advisable for situation.

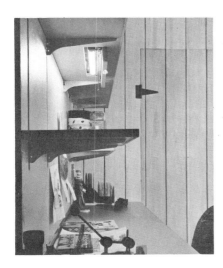

Small boy has well-designed desk and display case to grow with. Lumi-line tube hidden behind a facer board to avoid glare spreads light up and down across light-colored back surface; it is ideal for reading, drawing, model building.

TOM RILEY

ART HUPY

In basement room, ground-level window admits sunlight through slot in ceiling. Artificial light can repeat this play-table illumination at night.

DARROW WATT

During remodel, little girl's room acquired closet space, a "bay-window" seat with fluorescent soffit lighting by building out from an existing flat wall.

THE WELL-LIGHTED READER

Reading, that most pleasurable and informative of man's activities and the one you now pursue, places great demands upon your eyes. Paper can be polished and shiny. Type can be close-set and tiny. A long stretch of serious reading improperly lighted invites a resounding headache. For a young student, poor lighting may mean serious vision trouble in the future.

Because reading is so important a part of contemporary living, lighting experts have paid extraordinary attention to lighting the pages of a book. Their recommendations are the result of careful studies.

Easy chair reading requires no more than one portable lamp in an otherwise well-lighted room.

R. WENKAM

This den is ideally equipped for armchair reading. The floor lamp, placed at a back corner of the arm chair, has a large shade with good light transmitting properties. Diffusing bowl shields 300-watt bulb. Cove lighting above the book wall provides good general illumination level. Floor is light background.

The reading lamp should have a power of 250 to 300 watts, diffused by a bowl or by a disc at the bottom of the shade. A shade 18 inches in diameter at its lower edge, 10 inches in diameter at the top, and 10 inches deep, will spread light enough to avoid too-dark background. The lower edge of the shade should be 47 inches above the floor if the lamp is at a rear corner of the chair, and 40 inches above the floor if alongside.

Serious reading and studying are best done at a desk designed for the purpose. A properly set up study area entails more than the placing of light fixtures. One industry study group notes these requirements: Light spread evenly across the work surface; absence of shadows from hands or body; no direct view of bulbs in lighting fixtures or extreme brightness at bottom of shade; no glare spot on lamp shades; a light-colored desk surface; a light-colored back wall or tack board (but never a window, because of changing glare patterns outside); some light cast up on walls or ceiling, and some general light elsewhere in the room. Also, shiny surfaces should be avoided if possible.

These conditions can be met with two wall-mounted or table lamps with diffusing bowls. Shades should be 15 inches in diameter, and 15 inches above the desk top. Space lamps 30 inches apart on centers, and use 150 watt bulbs. A fluorescent tube, shielded by a faceboard 5 inches deep, and placed 15 to 18 inches above the desk top also meets all requirements.

Above, sources used together are good for reading. Opaque top on wall fixture counteracted by soffit in corner. Tube light in desk also borrows from it.

Faintly whimsical suspended lamp meets requirements for reading. Overhead light source, spill light from other rooms through glass wall help local source.

MORLEY BAER

ERNEST BRAUN

Easy-to-arrange reading corner uses a table lamp with diffusing bowl, a large shade. It is close to dark wood wall to minimize contrasts.

Below, left, two lamps spaced 30 inches apart light desk properly. Note light screens that eliminate possible glare sources outdoors.

Below, a fluorescent tube is concealed in bottom of small storage cabinet. Tube 18 inches above desk top. Slot beams light upward.

GLENN CHRISTIANSEN

ERNEST BRAUN

R. WENKAM

MARTIN WEBER

The basic idea of the wall bracket is employed over this study desk to provide both functional and decorative light. The top of the bracket is covered by a sheet of diffusing plastic to form a shelf. Fred Langhorst design lights wall above desk, too.

GLENN CHRISTIANSEN

Unlike solution shown above, bookcase above the desk does not permit light to escape above. Overhead fixture used to compensate. Note large white blotter on dark desk top.

R. WENKAM

Large table lamp provides good work light for desk; uses diffusing bowl. Note hood lamps on book wall behind.

KITCHEN COUNTERS

The kitchen is above all others a functional room. It occupies the attention of a housewife, especially one with youngsters, for a good part of each day.

In the course of a year, the lady of the house more or less expects a few cuts from broken glass or can lids, and a burn or two for having gotten hold of the hot end of the pot. Each day in the kitchen she deals with sharp objects and hot ones. Often, she is distracted by toddler or telephone right in the middle of a task, or she continues to be sociable with guests as she goes about duties that become increasingly hurried as a major meal nears serving. In these difficult conditions, a woman should be able to see

Expansive kitchen painted in bright colors and white is lighted by large central fixture, and rows of fluorescent tubes mounted under cabinets. The tubes are shielded from view by depth of the cabinets. Central fixture spreads light in a uniform sphere, and is not in contrast with background. Vladimir Ossipoff design.

quickly and accurately where her hands are going next if she is going to keep the cuts and burns down to a tolerable number.

The luminous ceiling, once a purely commercial lighting device, became a part of residential lighting in the kitchen before it appeared in other parts of the home because it produces the shadowless, glare-free light that is needed for fast vision.

The kitchen, because it is mainly a work room, lends itself to the structural lighting devices that provide even and glare-free light. Luminous panels, cornices and similar units are alternatives to the fully luminous ceiling.

The basic light usually is overhead, to brighten traffic paths between the work areas (and to make the floor easier to clean). Important supplemental lights overhead or under cupboards should be located at the sink, at the range, and at any counter or table top where meat or other foods are carved or cut. Since many appliances and counter surfaces are of gloss or semi-gloss finish, diffusion is in most cases advisable.

One of the commonest glare-shadow sources is the counter space beneath overhanging cabinets. Strips of tube light mounted on the bottom of the cabinets at the rear solve the problem and add to the general illumination level.

In using fluorescent light in a kitchen, you may find it worthwhile to pay the premium price for the Deluxe warm white tubes. This type of tube provide the truest rendition of food colors. For more description of tube types, see pages 80-81.

ERNEST BRAUN

Above, direct-indirect fixtures mounted on wall light one side of pullman kitchen. Fluorescent tubes hidden under overhang light work surfaces at right in photo.

Two semi-recessed spotlights brighten pass-through counter. Ceiling-mounted diffusing cylinders are work and general light for other kitchen surfaces.

GEORGE KNIGHT

ERNEST BRAUN

DEARBORN-MASSAR

Honeycomb plastic eggcrate is the diffusing agent for soffit above kitchen sink, work counter. Note use of windows as backsplash in Terry & Moore design.

Left, a combination cove-and-soffit lights the areas near kitchen windows. An extended troffer provides general illumination. Reel lamp for breakfast table.

JULIUS SHULMAN

Spacious kitchen gets general illumination from series of reel lamps like one above table. The large plate in the wall at left lights two-step change of level coming into kitchen. A row of recessed incandescent units placed in the soffit over work counter gives good local light. Design is by Lockwood de Forest.

ERNEST BRAUN

In a pullman-type kitchen, two combination cove-and-soffit units provide both local and general illumination. This is an approach especially suited to lofty sloping ceiling in this home. The fields of light from the two units overlap to provide even light on floor, and brighten ceiling area. Design, Henrik Bull.

MARTIN WEBER

This cove-and-soffit, beneath a standard flat ceiling, gets better reflection from it than unit in photo above, so needs less downlight. Small panels are enough.

R. WENKAM

Recessed "eye-ball" units swivel in housings to give control over light direction. This type of soffit lighting needs supplemental lighting overhead.

GEORGE BALLIS

ARTCREST

Skylight unit contains incandescent lights above plastic diffusing panel, lights a small work counter at night.

Fully luminous ceiling, available in kit form, can be the sole source of light in a kitchen, unless exceptionally deep overhanging cabinets are used. Multi-directional light eliminates most shadows, glare spots.

ERNEST BRAUN

ERNEST BRAUN

Curved plastic shield for fluorescent tubes under cabinets minimizes possible glare on shiny surfaces. Manufactured unit is on market.

Incandescent bulbs above diffusing panels of skylight are general light source. Tubes under cabinets, recessed light over stove. Design is by Burde, Shaw, and Kearns.

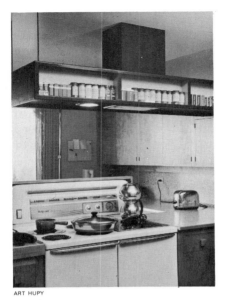

ART HUPY

Shelf built around ventilator holds downlight for stove, small bulbs to brighten the whole structure.

ART HUPY

During a remodel, owners extended kitchen wall to enlarge the room. The overhead space was made into a combination skylight and troffer, with wire glass above and plastic diffusers at ceiling height.

R. WENKAM

Barbecue designed for indoor or outdoor use is located between the kitchen and patio. When meal is to be eaten outdoors, wooden doors are folded back, permitting use of outdoor hanging lamp to supplement special heat resistant fixture mounted inside ventilator hood assembly.

HOBBY AND UTILITY LIGHTING

Your home may be, in addition to the matters already mentioned, a laundry, a garden work center, a carpenter's shop, a hobby and crafts center, and perhaps a music studio, a painter's garret and a table tennis arena as well.

All of these involve "work." Some of them require light so you can see what your hands are doing. Some of them require light so you can see the results of what you have done, or instructions for what you are about to do. Many of them require light for each of these purposes.

The type of light source you choose is governed by the physical size of the task, and by the speed with which it must be done or by the fineness of coordination it involves.

ERNEST BRAUN

Two long troffers with miniature egg-crate diffusers and a recessed luminous panel provide general and work light for studio-family room. Units are placed to shed strong downlight on all work surfaces. Egg-crates better than solid diffusers for this purpose. Note that floor provides low-contrast background.

STEVEN C. WILSON

Eye-ball units at regular intervals in ceiling are directional and general light. Troffer at wall aids background brightness, lights finished canvases.

CLYDE CHILDRESS

Commercial-type fluorescent fixtures are grouped to form luminous ceiling in studio. Hooded lamps (at left in photo) provide directional light for artist.

Table tennis, for example, should be highly illuminated if the players are skillful. The darting flight of the ball is difficult enough to follow without glare and shadow patterns to confound the issue. Fluorescent fixtures or ceiling recessed lights should cast even light over the area of the table top for maximum benefit.

Painting, especially if you linger among the representational artists, needs a high level of illumination to give colors their true value, and directional light to simulate the lighting in the scene you paint. Proper highlight and shadow effects can be extremely difficult to achieve if the light on the canvas fights with the light in the scene you wish to capture.

Most crafts work benches are best lighted by a broad source fixture, usually fluorescent tubes, located 48 inches above the work surface. The extended source sends light down from several directions, minimizing shadows on or around the work. Detail work can profit by a stronger directional light that can be trained on the area where it is most needed at the moment. For draftsmen, a hooded lamp on a hinged arm can supplement general overhead light. In a shop, ceiling-mounted cone or eyeball units are often useful.

Flower arranging can be done under almost any handy light, but an effort to match the lighting in the area where the arrangement will finally be displayed can give you a clearer idea of how it will look in place.

Laundries are not especially difficult to light. The problem is basically that of the work bench. However, to see clearly into the depths of the washer or dryer, the light should be located to do the job. With top-loading machines, the fixture can be directly over the machines. Front-loading models may be more efficiently lighted by locating the fixture over the area where you stand to load the machines.

Hobby and utility 57

R. WENKAM

R. WENKAM

ELIZABETH GREEN

Huge skylights in north wall provide daytime light in this studio. Suspended globes take over at night. Easels can be moved about to get light direction set.

Above left, troffer much like one on page 57 is designed to serve the same purpose. It is combined with a skylight for day or night illumination.

Large globe used for both directional and general light in this studio. Note the small fixture on wall behind, aimed to reflect light off skylight.

DARROW WATT

Bullet lamps mounted on bottom of overhead storage space can be aimed for strong work light wherever home handyman needs it. A sizeable luminous panel in true ceiling provides general illumination.

GLENN CHRISTIANSEN

Simple wall bracket with row of tube lights behind casts ample light on bench in a home work shop.

GLENN CHRISTIANSEN

Plastic diffusers over fluorescent tubes spread bright, even light over the work area in this shop. Eyeball units are interposed in these fixtures for strong directional light on heavy-duty machines.

GLENN CHRISTIANSEN

Similar units are over work bench in same shop. Note glass diffusers on eyeballs to minimize glare on work.

Hobby and utility 59

TOM BURNS JR.

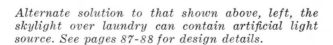

A long hallway used as a laundry is lighted by skylights during the day, and by ceiling-mounted fixtures at night. Note that diffusers spread light across ceiling.

Alternate solution to that shown above, left, the skylight over laundry can contain artificial light source. See pages 87-88 for design details.

WILLIAM APLIN

In large utility areas, this type of reel lamp (100-foot cord) is handy for temporary local light.

DARROW WATT

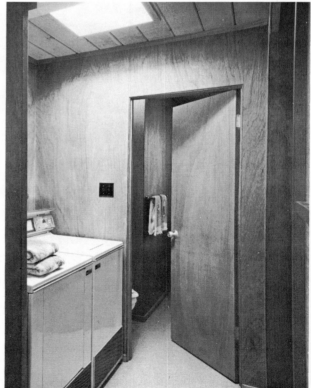

GLENN CHRISTIANSEN

A simple wall bracket attached to exposed rafters in carport lights laundry area, work bench. Note the raceway wiring on the wall for use with power tools.

ERNEST BRAUN

Bullet lamps mounted high on walls to avoid glare cast strong light on a flower arranging center. The light is similar to that in often-used display area.

DARROW WATT

Another approach to lighting a flower arranging counter. Fluorescent tubes are mounted behind 5-inch deep facer 18 inches above the work surface.

Sewing center gets local light from fluorescent tubes under pigeon-hole cabinet. General light from soffit reflects off light colored doors when they are shut.

ROY KRELL

Hobby and utility 61

*A row of hooded spotlights are **both** decorative and useful over yarn rack. Loom lighted by other fixtures.*

DEARBORN-MASSAR

GEORGE BALLIS

A single eyeball unit mounted in the ceiling directly above a piano bench illuminates score brightly and evenly, and is far enough away to provide broad pool of light. General lighting should be good.

DEARBORN-MASSAR

Combination skylight and troffer with fluorescent tubes provides excellent light for young piano student.

CHAS. R. PEARSON

Lighting THE EXTERIOR

WELCOMING ENTRYWAYS

Guests arriving at a house at night want to know immediately where the front door is, and to feel secure about getting to it. Even more basic, they want to be sure it is your door on a first visit.

An entryway is designed to provide a safe and inviting means of access to a house, and as a signature for it. Lighting should be designed to preserve these qualities after dark. The entryway also serves as a transition between the night outdoors and the bright indoors.

Most manufactured entry lights are designed to cast a broad pool of light down to the ground, where it is needed by someone mounting stairs, or walking on a narrow and perhaps irregular surface. They are carefully shielded to avoid harsh light in the eyes of approaching guests, because glare will impair their vision of the path before them. Both these requirements can also be met well by glass or plastic diffusing panels that let light spill out onto the porch or step from indoors.

If your landscaping permits, you need not rely on fixtures attached to the house wall or to the entry overhead. Spotlights mounted in trees and aimed toward the entryway can achieve a dramatic effect at no cost in efficiency. They

CAMERA HAWAII

Main living areas of house front on street. Architect Frank Slavsky uses light to gain privacy from passers by as well as to welcome guests. Spot under eave lights walk; others behind plastic panels to left of door create interesting shadows of plant forms. Louvers over windows let light filter out across face of house.

should be used carefully, however, so that persons leaving the house are not blinded by their powerful beams.

There are two minor points worth thought. The world is full of houses with street numbers that are badly lit, or not lit at all. In many cases, they are the handiest identifying mark for a first-time guest during the day, but the last source of help at night. A helpful entry lighting scheme will include proper display of the house number. Numerals three inches high can be read by a standing person at 75 feet. A car, however, would have to stop.

Second, insects are less attracted by yellow light than by blue. The yellower the light, the less attraction. Gas light attracts few insects, but provides a warm and cheery light that is attractive to people.

As a matter of convenience, outdoor fixtures should be designed so maintenance can be done with a minimum of difficulty.

CHAS. R. PEARSON

Plastic panels also can be used as reflectors. A row of cone lamps in carport eaves lights surface of panels; indoor light from behind. Kenneth Bates, designer.

MARVIN RAND

Indoor garden uses general light from living room to create drama with fatshedera shadows on plastic panels. City house entry design by Killingsworth, Brady & Smith.

R. WENKAM

CLYDE CHILDRESS

CLYDE CHILDRESS

A series of spotlights shine up from ground, through bamboo to light way to door. Small recessed fixture over door can be used separately if desired.

Above, left, lumiline tubes recessed between double beams light step up at entry. Direct-indirect fixture over door to living room; spot above tree.

Low-voltage lighting system uses six lamps to light entry garden, walkway. Three units visible, under trees at right, in tub. One lamp outside the gate.

66 Exterior

ERNEST BRAUN

Immense suspended cage with diffusing cylinder of plastic inside provides an intriguing introduction and lights wide area around entry for arrivals.

TOM RILEY

Globe suspended from porch ceiling is basic light for entry, but Christmas bulbs in used plastic bleach bottles help light the walk for party guests.

ERNEST BRAUN

A smaller entryway light works in same way as unit in photo above. Plastic diffuser spreads soft light over wide area.

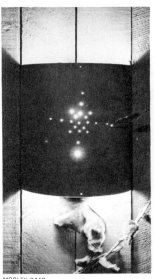

MORLEY BAER

WILLIAM APLIN

Two similar custom-designed units for mounting on walls at entry areas. In photo at left, curved sheet of perforated metal; at right, wood. Cut-away tin can shields bulbs, helps direct light down.

Entryways 67

UTILITY LIGHT

There are, with most houses, a number of outdoor areas that require utility light for the convenience of the family as they go about their normal daily routines. Back doors, carports, walks, and, on large lots, out-buildings all may need light fixtures for night-time use.

Your choices of fixtures for these locations may in part be governed by the frequency with which guests may use the areas in question, although in most cases economy and utility are the main points to consider.

While front doors are lighted to welcome guests, other doors reserved for family use can often be less brightly illuminated. Also, the lighted area need not be so large. Recessed ceiling lights of small dimensions can adequately light a small porch and a short flight of stairs leading to it. Many of these manufactured units use only a single 60 or 75 watt bulb. A lift-out glass plate makes replacing light bulbs easy. Small, glass-bowl fixtures are also available. Many of them have two set screws holding the bowl in place over a medium-wattage bulb. Others are open at the bottom for easy re-lamping. As is the case with formal entry fixtures, sources should be diffused to avoid glare, especially if there are steps or other changes of level near the door.

Carports can be sufficiently lighted by a single

MORLEY BAER

DARROW WATT

Simple and effective lighting system for under-house carport uses a frosted globe over 100-watt bulb mounted on carport ceiling, and a similar wall-mounted unit over right side of driveway (in vines).

Two variations on the low-mounted downlight are designed to spread light over walk, flower border.

fixture suspended from the rafters three or more feet above the center of the car roof. It is better in some cases to have lights arranged so they illuminate the floor near each door of the parked car, to make loading and unloading easier. In two-car carports, a row of three lamps across the rafters will provide light of this type.

A closed garage, in addition to this type of lighting in the interior, may need another fixture mounted on the outside wall above the main door so a night arrival can see to unlock it.

Walkways should always be lighted either by spotlights mounted under the eaves, or by low-to-the-ground units that spread all their light down, such as mushroom fixtures, or wall-recessed louvered lights. Any source that shines light in the eyes of a person using the walk is a potential hazard. Post lamps on front walks should have diffusing panes around the light source, whether it is electric or gas. It is a convenience to have all outdoor utility lights equipped with three-way switches so they can be turned on or off from inside the house, or at the source. This is particularly true of carport or garage lights. Switches in carports or garages should be located so you do not have to walk far to reach them after getting out of the car in the dark (unless you don't mind leaving the car lights on while you get to the switch).

ERNEST BRAUN

Custom-built light for walkway is redwood box mounted on corner of brick wall. Placed to shine on steps. Slot allows light to glow on small statue above.

WILLIAM APLIN

Recessed louvered lights, used here in a patio wall, can be used to light walks along any wall or fence.

RICHARD DAWSON

A low-voltage, waterproof unit 8 inches long is one of series from parking area to front door of house.

MAYNARD L. PARKER

Open-topped redwood frame with frosted glass front makes efficient porch light for utility entryway.

Carports and walks 69

ON THE PATIO

All the qualities that make the patio or terrace an enviable possession on a summer afternoon also make it an attractive place to spend a warm summer evening. It is an informal, comfortable, and naturally ventilated room where you can relax, or enjoy a party in the freedom of the outdoors.

Though it is in many ways a room, the patio often does not have walls and a ceiling that reflect light in the way indoors surfaces do. When it does not have them, the approach to lighting will be different than that employed indoors.

Outdoor living areas seldom need to be brightly illuminated. Parties, or simple outdoor sitting do not involve any critical vision. You need only to see the people you are with, and be

JOHN HARTLEY

Custom-designed patio lights are made of perforated brass frames, plastic diffusing panels bolted on sides. Single 75-watt bulb in each unit. Fixtures faced to minimize bright light shining in through house windows; also minimize reflection in windows from indoor lights, extend space. Design, Knowlton Ferland, Jr.

able to get around without running into furniture or stepping into planters.

A frequently used solution is the spot or flood light mounted above the patio, under an eave or in a tree, and directed toward the patio floor. Lighting experts recommend that the lamps be mounted at least 14 feet above the patio floor so they will not be in the line of vision, and aimed at an angle ranging from vertical to 45° (but not toward a neighbor's window), so shadows will not be too long. Extremely long shadows distort objects and create illusion that can cause mis-steps or falls. Two lamps serve better than one to eliminate deep shadows, if used far enough apart. A PAR-38 floodlamp of 150 watts, mounted 15 feet above the patio and aimed at an angle of 45° will cast a soft, fairly even light over an area 56 feet long and 32 feet wide. A similar spotlight arrangement will cast brighter light over an area 18 feet long and 12 feet wide. Lamps aimed straight down produce a much smaller area of light.

If you have some type of translucent overhead, flood or spot lights can be mounted three to four feet above it and aimed through it. The number and placement is governed by the amount of light and the evenness you wish. One 150-watt flood centered 3 feet above each 4-foot square of overhead will provide a bright and fairly even illumination through plastic panels, or sheets.

Patios outside window walls sometimes can be lighted by light spilling from an indoor room. In most cases some ornamental lamps on the patio itself will create a cozier atmosphere, and diminish shadows on the garden side. There are both wall-mounted and floor lamps designed especially for outdoor use (see page 94). The popular suspended globes also serve the pur-

DON NORMARK

CLYDE CHILDRESS

Above, pottery lamps suspended from pipe (containing wiring) make cheerful light on screen, patio. Basic light is PAR floodlight in eaves. Design, Bert Perry.

Curved sheets of copper mounted on posts supporting patio roof provide up and down light. Reflection off solid roof painted white spreads light well.

CLYDE CHILDRESS

A row of fluorescent tubes in waterproof boxes makes deck patio bright, cheerful. Units are recessed in spaces between double beams. Incandescent lights with diffusers can achieve similar effect. In any solution of this type, reflecting shield above source is essential, or 50% of light lost. Design, Goodwin Steinberg.

ERNEST BRAUN

Six 150-watt PAR lamps outside lath fence are aimed to shine into overhanging Eucalyptus trees; they also glow through spaces between laths to light patio.

pose. The globes should diffuse light more thoroughly than typical indoor lamps since they may often be seen against a black background. Lamps of these types may also be used to light an entire patio.

Plastic or other diffusing screens can be used as diffusing agents for PAR or other reflector lamps placed at or near ground level behind them. This approach offers the opportunity to use dramatic silhouettes against the glowing panels as a decorative device. The reverse, shining the lamps onto the face of the panels, will provide reflected light for the patio.

In considering a patio lighting scheme, you may want to look into the cheery flame light offered by natural gas fixtures. They are as practical as electric lamps for patio use, if your home is equipped for gas service. Open flame torches and traditional post lamps are available. Types of gas lights are described on page 95.

DARROW WATT

ERNEST BRAUN

Large diffusing globe suspended from patio overhead supplements light from indoors, reduces deep shadows.

Gas-fired luau torches create atmosphere of campfire on patio adjoining a swimming pool. Each unit has lever valve near base to control flame. Spotlights on ground behind bench add to illumination level.

RICHARD FISH

CLYDE CHILDRESS

Patio detached from house uses a series of globes suspended from trees to achieve fairly high illumination level. Light-colored screen in background is good reflecting agent, helps reduce sharp contrasts.

A single spotlight above canvas panel gives even, soft light. Idea can be used with any translucent overhead.

THE LUMINOUS GARDEN

Lighting a garden at night is a luxury. It is not necessary to health or well-being. But it can be a beautiful luxury, and it need not be

WILLIAM APLIN

The photographs show the contrast between a garden during the day and the same garden at night. Each photo is shot so that the left half is open, and the right half through a glass sliding door, to show how night garden lighting removes reflections from windows. All but one of spotlights are mounted beyond wall.

unbearably expensive. Some of the benefits have a useful side, too.

Lighting the garden, for all practical purposes, gives you two gardens to enjoy. The sun-bathed garden of afternoon looks much different than one selectively lighted by artificial lamps. A lighted garden can decorate the "walls" of the patio, an outdoor room that can benefit as much from decorative light as a living room. The lighted garden can offer a night-time view through picture windows or window walls that otherwise must be covered by draperies, or left as black rectangles that swallow light rather than provide it. A garden of lighted pathways can let you stroll at a leisurely pace in the cool of evening, to enjoy the beauty and the heady perfume that many plants breathe into still night air.

Like most other decorative lighting, plant lighting is governed by a few, general rules. The main caution is to use light sparingly. Artificial light, versatile as it has become, cannot compete with the sun. An evenly lighted garden is pale and flat-appearing at night. On the other hand, a few bold plants lighted to dramatize shape or texture can create a sense of depth in a small garden.

Of course lights should be located so they do not shine into a neighbor's window, or directly in the eyes of anyone in the garden. Glare outdoors is a more difficult problem to put up with than it is indoors because backgrounds to a light source will usually be black.

The basis of garden lighting is the matching of light to shape and texture of a plant or a group of plants. The following partial list may give you hints for types of plants to light and ways to light them.

TREES

Japanese maple. A small, delicate tree, it has a stepped or shingled appearance that lends itself to a soft, diffused light placed at its base. A mature tree can be lighted by soft light placed at one side to illuminate it from tip to bottom.

Birch. Its small leaves, open and drooping branches, and white bark pick up any light. Even moonlight or house lights will dot leaves with silver and accentuate branches. Try a very subdued light under birch trees, or a slightly stronger light hidden behind nearby full shrubs.

Brazilian pepper. A spreading tree with soft, feathery foliage that cascades from irregular and gnarled branches, it allows light placed directly beneath to filter out in fern-like patterns. The light can be spread over a greater part of the tree if it is tucked among the highest branches and aimed downward.

Aacias. The graceful, weeping *Acacia pendula* lends itself to silhouette treatment against a tall building or a skyline. Hidden spotlights that shine up through foliage to reveal its shape are one treatment. The soft, silvery *Acacia Baileyana* is almost self-illuminating. Try a floodlight on the side of the house or atop a fence to enhance its nebulous, cloudy form.

Weeping willow. The shape and continual activity of breeze-stirred branches make it a good subject for even flood-lighting of an entire side. Many trees reflect well in water with night lighting, but the cascading willow is especially suited.

Liquidambar. A dense-foliaged, upright growing tree with minimum spread, it lends itself to "brush" lighting (as do many evergreens). Place strong spotlights on the ground a few feet away from the tree, and aim them so they light only the outer tips of limbs on one side to achieve a chiseled effect of light and deep black.

SHRUBS

Azara. Soft, filtered light enhances the delicate, lace-like foliage of the plant. For delicate

CLYDE CHILDRESS

WILLIAM APLIN

A single spotlight mounted at right so it cannot be seen through window makes tree seem self-illuminated. Note shadow patterns on driftwood in foreground.

At left, a similar approach to one shown above focuses attention on the trunk of a more densely foliaged tree. Light source is closer to tree base.

CLYDE CHILDRESS

Nearest approach to sunlight, a flood lamp above the plant (in this case an aralia used as a demonstrator).

A spotlight located in much the same way as a floodlight will dramatize one cluster of leaves on a plant.

Backlight from below dramatic because it seldom occurs in nature. Best with translucent leaves.

shadow patterns, place light directly at the base of the plant. For wispy outline effects, place them at a distance.

Bamboo. A small amount of light goes a long way with bamboo. One effective treatment is the placing of a group of ground lights in the center of a clump, with each light turned in a slightly different direction than its neighbor. Bamboo has a pleasingly eerie appearance when it is lighted by open flame, such as gas-fed luau torches. But open flame should be kept a good distance from the plants as they burn easily.

Tree ferns. When softly lighted from below, they can capture the feeling of an entire garden, even if no other plants are lighted. Tiny shadows and sparkles weave over its foliage and filter out onto nearby structures and plants.

Acanthus. Because of its large, sculptured leaves, it is most spectacular if you light it in such a way that its foliage is silhouetted against light. Use small lights, even flashlights; you may want a reflecting background such as a fence. Shining light through plastic panels can make it soft enough.

Ferns. To emphasize the fine, delicate foliage, light them from beneath. Small lights are best if you wish to avoid glare. The open nature of the plants does not hide a light source well.

Sedum. Taller growing varieties, such as *Sedum proealtum*, grow in a tangled fashion that can be effectively lighted by a diffused light hidden among the plants or in the background.

Silhouetting shows shape and outline of a plant. It is best used with bold forms. Panel behind plant is lighted.

Shadows are striking by-product of light. Here, shadow on light colored panel is more decorative than plant.

FRANK L. GAYNOR

Tree which is not too dense can be lighted from below with success. Photo above shows location of vapor-proof fixture. At left, the result.

CLYDE CHILDRESS

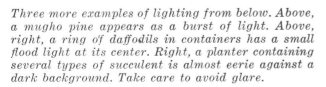

CLYDE CHILDRESS

CLYDE CHILDRESS

Three more examples of lighting from below. Above, a mugho pine appears as a burst of light. Above, right, a ring of daffodils in containers has a small flood light at its center. Right, a planter containing several types of succulent is almost eerie against a dark background. Take care to avoid glare.

CLYDE CHILDRESS

ERNEST BRAUN

ERNEST BRAUN

Another example of lighting a light colored panel for silhouette effect. Raised bed at rear property line.

Above right, a mushroom reflector mounted on fence post casts highlights on plants of dramatic shape.

Floodlight treatment of an open tree from a point below and to one side can produce even more delicate shape than tree has in daylight, especially if light brushes one side.

GLENN CHRISTIANSEN

Materials and Construction

MATERIALS AND CONSTRUCTION

| A BULB (STANDARD) | G BULB (GLOBULAR) | T BULB (TUBULAR) | S BULB (STRAIGHT-SIDED) | PS BULB (PEAR-SHAPED) |

Once you have decided in general what sort of lighting you wish to have, there remain the questions of specific lamp and fixture types, and the operating aspects. This chapter describes the range of choices in each of these areas, and ways to plan installations of those choices.

TYPES OF LIGHT

Incandescent light, the major type in use in American homes since Thomas Alva Edison, is the product of the glow from a fine wire filament heated by electric current.

The resulting light has a warm color value. (The yellow color suggests warmth because it resembles the color of sunlight.) Incandescent light intensifies warm colors in a decorating scheme. Although it mutes cool colors, the change is not evident or annoying.

Because of the structure and size of the bulb and filament, most incandescent light lends itself to point or spot lighting. Light coming from a small source works best in a small area. Of course incandescent bulbs can be used in clusters or rows to provide a larger "source."

The first incandescent bulbs were of clear glass. They produced a hot, harsh light that spread in all directions from the filament, which was clearly visible through the glass. Today, you can buy bulbs that diffuse the light and soften it, or ones that intensify the light and direct it.

There are several common bulb shapes available for general interior use in portable or mounted fixtures. They are referred to by a code letter-number (A-19, PS-25). The letter indicates shape (see sketch). The number shows maximum dimension in eighths of an inch. The inside-frosted bulb, most common type in current use, is the one which shows a faint image of its filament near the center. The white bulb, a more

recent development, diffuses the light evenly and shows no image of the filament. Tinted bulbs in pink, yellow, green, aqua, and blue are made in the same way as white bulbs, but they produce somewhat less light. The main value is decorative. The warm colors intensify a warm decorating scheme, or subdue a cool one. The cool tints have the reverse effect. Neutral paints can be made either warm or cool by these bulbs.

The general use bulbs come in wattages of 15, 25, 30, 40, 50, 60, 75, 100, 150, and 200. Three-light bulbs are available in 30-70-100, 50-100-150, and 50-200-250 sizes with medium bases, and in 50-100-150 and 100-200-300-watt sizes with mogul (the largest) bases.

There are in addition to these general purpose bulbs a number of incandescent types which are essentially decorative. At one end of the decorative light spectrum are the flood and spot lights. Unlike general-use bulbs, they direct light through the expanded end of the bulb. Flood lights have a coat of reflecting silver on the sides and a fairly heavily frosted tip which diffuses the light. Spot lights are similar, except that the frost coat is lighter and less diffusing. They are used to wash relatively large objects or areas with a more intense light than other bulb types would give. Medium base R or PAR bulbs are available in wattages from 30 to 300. The R bulbs are made of the same glass as other general-use

bulbs. Outdoors, they must be shielded from the weather. The PAR (for parabolic) bulbs are made of hard glass especially suited to exposed outdoor use. Both R and PAR lamps come in red, yellow, green and blue, as well as untinted glass.

At the other extreme are the "broad-source" incandescent lamps. The lumiline tube, an incandescent type similar in appearance and purpose to fluorescent tubes, is another means of getting a wash of light. The tubes are an inch in diameter, and come in 30-, 40-, 60-watt sizes, with clear or frosted tubing. They are roughly one-fifth as bright as their fluorescent counterparts. The color value is warmer than any fluorescent. They require special disc sockets.

A smaller source is the showcase light. Available in 30-, 40-, and 60-watts, the medium base tube is used primarily to light paintings, small sculpture, or other art objects.

Incandescent lamps of all types generate considerably more heat than do fluorescent tubes. The average life is roughly 750 burning hours. The general-use bulbs provide one-fourth to one-third as much light per watt as fluorescents.

Introduced in 1938, the fluorescent tube did not find its way into the home in numbers until after World War II, when architectural design moved in new directions and tube qualities improved considerably for residential uses.

The principle is quite different from incandescent lighting. Tiny filaments at either end of the tube bombard mercury gas with electrons. The ultra-violet light produced is changed to visible light by a phosphor powder coating on the inside of the tube. (In new tubes, the coating is not dangerous, as it was in earlier models.)

The fluorescent tube provides a line of light rather than a point of it. The long line lends itself to relatively large fields of light, useful both for general illumination and work light. The extended field reduces directional shadows and glare.

Fluorescent tubes, higher priced than incandescent bulbs, yield three to four times as much light per watt, have an average life of 7,500 burning hours, and operate at lower temperatures. Brightness levels cannot be changed as easily. Any medium base incandescent bulb can be substituted for any other. But the entire fluorescent fixture must be changed in most cases to get a new illumination level. This is because the surface area of the tube is directly related to its output of light. For this reason it is advisable to seek the advice of an experienced dealer or electrician before buying and installing fluorescent fixtures.

Fluorescent tubes come in several white color values, of which all but one can be used successfully in the home. However, it is not advisable to mix different whites in one room because they do not blend together, but create a patchwork effect. The choices:

Improved-color-rendition warm white (called Deluxe) is not as bright as standard warm white, but gives a better rendition of food and human coloring. It blends well with incandescent light, and so serves well in areas where both decorative light and coloring are important.

Improved-color-rendition cool white, the counterpart of the improved warm white tube, does not go as well with incandescent light, but in the right place gives a pleasingly cool light that enhances cool colors in a decorative scheme.

Warm white, the standard home lighting tube until the improved types appeared, is about 25% brighter than they are, but it has a slight adverse effect on both warm and cool colors. It is a good work light for utility areas.

Cool white, the other standard, intensifies cool colors and dulls warm ones.

White, a compromise between warm and cool whites, slightly dulls the appearance of warm colors.

Daylight-color tubes are very seldom used in homes because the blue-white light produces a chill atmosphere and grays human complexions.

Soft white gives off a pink light that emphasizes reds and pinks, but tends to gray cool colors.

Fluorescent light is also available in pink, red, blue and gold. Color is used primarily in carefully designed decorative displays rather than for any general purpose.

In addition to color distinctions, fluorescent light units are separated by their starting methods. There are three types, pre-heat, rapid-start, and trigger-start. A fourth and universal type is called the pre-heat-rapid-start. The pre-heat fixture assembly includes a small metal canister, called the starter, which functions as a control. It is replaceable. The pre-heat tube requires several seconds to light fully. The rapid-start does not have a starter, but requires rapid-start tubes and ballasts. (Some pre-heat tubes will fit rapid-start fixtures, but will not light in them.) Trigger-start fixtures have special ballasts, and require trigger-start tubes. The newer pre-heat-rapid-start tubes will work in either the pre-heat or rapid-start fixture, but they do not light immediately in pre-heat fixtures.

Still another type of tube, the slimline, is seldom used in homes because it requires bulky sockets and a special, heavy ballast.

All fluorescent fixtures have a ballast, which is a current regulating device that can be mounted either in the channel, or "remoted" to a location in a cellar or attic. Fluorescent tubes require very high voltage to start, but taper off to a figure roughly in line with normal house currents. The ballast absorbs this fluctuation.

Ballasts are remoted for two reasons: to reduce channel weight so fixtures can be attached to valance or cornice faceboards, and avoid hum. Hum is not ordinarily audible, but can be heard in unusually quiet rooms. Remoted ballasts should be enclosed in an approved insulating shield, and should be ventilated to dissipate heat.

Fluorescent tubes come in a wide range of sizes, but all types are not universally available in all sizes. The smaller tubes, for example, may be obtainable only in the pre-heat type. The sizes:

4-watt T-5, 6-inch length, miniature bipin base;

6-watt T-5, 9-inch length, miniature bipin base;

8-watt T-5, 12-inch length, miniature bipin base;

13-watt T-5, 21-inch length, miniature bipin base;

14-watt T-12, 15-inch length, medium bipin base;

15-watt T-8, 18-inch length, medium bipin base;

20-watt T-12, 24-inch length, medium bipin base;

25-watt T-12, 33-inch length, medium bipin base;

30-watt T-8, 36-inch length, medium bipin base;

30-watt T-12, 36-inch length, medium bipin base;

and 40-watt T-12, 48-inch length, medium bipin base.

Circline lamps, universal pre-heat-rapid-start tubes, are currently on the market in three sizes:

22-watt T-9, outside diameter 8¼ inches; 32-watt T-10, outside diameter 12 inches; and 40-watt T-10, outside diameter 16 inches.

Fluorescent tubes, incidentally, can produce interference in radio reception. The interference can be eliminated by locating the radio and its antenna at a distance of nine or more feet from the nearest tube, or by installing interference filters on the radio.

TYPES OF FIXTURES

There are, without ignoring the several definitions offered in the first chapter, three basic approaches to lighting a room. There are wall lighting techniques, ceiling lighting techniques, and portable lighting techniques, which last borrows something from each of the others, and is more versatile.

WALL LIGHTING

Wall-lighting techniques, which include valances, wall-brackets, cornices, ceiling-mounted spot or flood lights, and luminous panels, are especially practical in open plan homes where interior spaciousness defeats conventional centered ceiling fixtures. As decorative light, any of these techniques are compatible with any architectural style if designed to match other aspects of the room. A valance faceboard in a functional home, for example, fits best if it is simple and clean in line. In a home with mullioned windows and Louis XV furniture, it might better be cut with scallops or swags.

The ease with which any of these wall-lighting units can be included in a remodel depends for the most part on the adaptability of the existing wiring. The carpentry involved in building any of them is not difficult. The expense is similarly dependent on the capacity of your wiring.

Valance

Before the industrial revolution attained its present complete state, a valance was the frilly top piece of a hanging of drapes. In modern lighting parlance, it is a shield for an extended line of indirect light placed above windows so it reflects from draperies drawn at night.

Most commonly, the valance is found in glass-walled rooms where light is needed for large draped surfaces. An example of the valance in use is on page 17.

Among the easiest of the structural lighting devices to add during a minor remodel, valance lighting involves only a small amount of carpentry. The major element is a faceboard to hide the light source. The board can be of any decorative design or material on its outer side. Manufactured metal and plastic models are available. Wooden faceboards are usually of ¾-inch (1-inch nominal) lumber. The inside face should be painted flat white to obtain the best reflection of light. Some light on the outer face from another source, or through translucent plastic, will prevent the faceboard from appearing as a too-dark silhouette. The lighter in color the board is, the easier it is to solve this small problem.

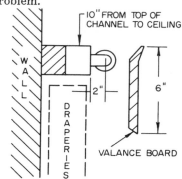

If the top of the faceboard is 12 inches from the ceiling, you should experience no harsh band of light above it. If the distance must be less than 10 inches, the top space should be enclosed by a dust cap, or the valance abandoned in favor of a cornice to avoid glare.

In most cases the faceboard is vertical, but it can be tilted out at top or bottom or both to a maximum of 20° to spread light over a larger area. Tilting out at the top helps spread light if the distance to the ceiling is less than 12 inches. Tilt-

ing it out at the bottom reflects more light back onto draperies with deep folds.

The board itself should be a minimum of 6 inches deep to hide the source properly. If the lower edge is more than 6 feet off the floor, this rule of thumb will adequately shield tubes from view: Equal distance from floor to board (measured in feet) with depth of faceboard (measured in inches). In short, if the distance from floor to faceboard is 8 feet, the faceboard should be 8 inches deep. For this formula to work, the top of the fixture channel should be even with the top of the faceboard. If furniture is close to the lighted wall, a "return" (lip) may be necessary to help keep light out of guests' eyes.

Swags, scallops, or other sawed designs should exceed these minimums rather than cut into them.

The distance from wall to faceboard may vary slightly, mainly to accommodate different drapery types, but the basic distance is 6 inches. The distance from wall to the center (long axis) of the tube should be a minimum of 4 inches, or as much more as you need to keep the tube center 2 inches from the draperies. If the tube is closer, light will not spread properly. On the other side, keep a distance of two inches from tube center to faceboard to make replacing lamps easy.

If you use regularly mounted tubes, you may need wood blocking between the fixture channel and the wall to obtain good results. Side-mounted tubes do not need blocking, unless you have deep-fold draperies.

If you use fixtures with the ballasts mounted in the channels, they should be mounted on the wall. Fixtures with remote ballasts, and lumi-line tubes can be mounted on the faceboard itself.

Use ½-inch strap iron of the length you need to attach the faceboard to the wall. Strap iron secured to the window header on 3-foot centers, or at every other stud will provide a sturdy support. Screws, of course, are sturdier than nails, but either will do.

The color of draperies and ceiling, and the type of drapery fold affects the light you get from a valance. The flat-folded types (box or cartridge pleats) present the most efficient reflecting surface. Deeper folds (French) swallow a good part of the light near the source. Colors should fall in the normal range of ceiling and wall reflectance values (see page 6) if you want a bright effect.

As a matter of convenience, choose tubes of equal length to fill a space. It will simplify matters when you buy new tubes. The total length of a row should be no more than a foot shorter than the faceboard to avoid contrasting dark edges (a short fill-in tube will not cause a variation in brightness levels). Center the line of tubes between the ends of the faceboard to avoid having one end seem brighter than the other. For the evenest spread of light, mount the channels end to end so there is the least possible separation between tube ends in the row. A small gap can cause a dark spot on the drapes.

To avoid having the drapery headings interfere with light above the valance, place the hooks as near the top as possible so the headings will not fold over toward the light tube.

Wall Brackets

A slight variation on the valance, the wall bracket can be used for either functional or decorative light. It is distinguished from the valance mainly in that it is not used with windows and draperies. Because it is not required to perch atop the window frame, it may be mounted at any height, and may be of any length. Mounted 65 inches or slightly higher above the floor, the wall bracket can be used to light lounge furniture, cabinetry, or informal dining tables. In shorter lengths and lower positions, it can be used to light desk tops, headboards for beds, or kitchen work surfaces.

The distance from the center of the long axis of the tube to the wall should be 4 inches, as is the case with valances. But the fixture channel can be attached at several heights behind the faceboard, depending on the distance from floor to faceboard. If the board is about 65 inches from the floor, the channels can be centered behind it. At lower altitudes, the channel can be mounted 2 inches above the lower edge of the faceboard.

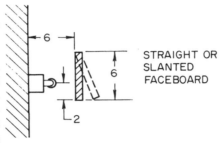

STRAIGHT OR SLANTED FACEBOARD

The faceboard itself should be no less than 5 inches deep in any case. If it is high on a wall, use the formula for valances. There are manufactured units available, completely wired and ready to install. If you wish to make your own, the specifications for valances again are suitable.

The wall bracket can easily be converted to a lighted display shelf by the addition of a diffusing plastic or glass top. The approach is especially practical if the bracket is below eye level for a standing person.

Used to light desks, the brackets should be designed to cast light up so there is no oppressive dark spot above the desk.

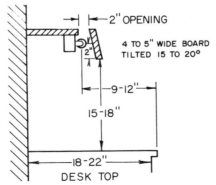

2" OPENING

4 TO 5" WIDE BOARD TILTED 15 TO 20°

9-12"

15-18"

18-22"

DESK TOP

Cornice

The cornice is in essence a ceiling mounted valance, which directs all of its light downward rather than letting an intense light fill a small area near the ceiling line. The cornice serves well to light drapery-covered walls or standard walls, and it is among the most effective solutions to lighting a book wall.

The faceboard is attached to the ceiling rather than to the wall, and the light channels are also mounted on the ceiling. The inside of the board should be painted flat white. The channel should be mounted so the center of the light tube is a minimum of 4 inches from a standard wall, or so it is 2 inches ahead of draperies. On the other side, 2 inches of space between the center of the tube and the inside of the faceboard will make tube replacement easy.

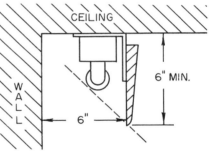

CEILING

WALL

6" MIN.

6"

The minimum depth of a cornice faceboard is 6 inches, if the channel is mounted on the faceboard (remoted ballast or lumiline tubes). If channel is mounted on ceiling, add the depth of the channel to the basic figure. If you use double rows of tubes for utilitarian light, the minimum depth is 8 inches.

Like valances, rooms with very high ceilings may require even deeper faceboards. The same rule of thumb applies, except that you should add an extra inch for channel depth or double rows of tubes as indicated in the preceding paragraph.

If the depth of the faceboard threatens to become clumsy, a return may be used to narrow the space between faceboard and wall.

The faceboard should be attached

to rafters. If the rafters run at right angles to the wall you are lighting, you can use screws at every other rafter. The screws should sink at least 2 inches into the rafter for strength. If the rafters run parallel to the wall you are lighting, you may be caught between. In this case, the easiest solution is to attach a wood blocking strip to the rafter nearest the wall, and to secure the faceboard to this strip, which should be wide enough to give you proper spacing between wall and faceboard.

The wood strip will prevent any light leaks above the faceboard. This problem can also be averted with a strip of decorative molding, or a strip of white felt used as a sealing cushion between faceboard and ceiling.

Spot and Floodlights

The lines of light described in the preceding sections are not the only ways to light a wall or draperies. There are a number of incandescent fixtures using the R and PAR type bulbs which can be used successfully to create even washes of light, or to make patterns of light and dark on a wall.

The typical units are cone or bullet lamps, attached to the ceiling, and the recessed or semi-recessed ceiling fixtures known as eye balls. Each has a swivelling action that permits some control over the direction of light. Installation requirements vary from one model to another, but the manufacturer's specifications are designed to give uniform light. To achieve uneven effects for decoration, install the units closer to the wall, or space them at increased distances.

You can fashion a somewhat less flexible wall lighting scheme of your own by recessing small lamp housings in a ceiling.

The housings should be ventilated to allow heat to dissipate into the attic, or elsewhere into the plenum (the space between the false ceiling and the true ceiling). The use of re-

flective metal surfaces inside the cavity will help intensify the light, but flat white paint may be enough.

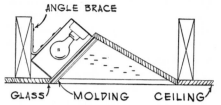

Luminous Walls

There is the reverse approach. You can make a wall or a panel in a wall a source of light in itself. Luminous wall panels can be used almost anywhere in the home. The effect is of a shaded window in daylight, which makes the device especially suitable in interior kitchens or baths. They can also be used in cases where privacy needs do not permit an ordinary window, or where a long expanse of wall would look better with a window, but structure does not permit one. Finally, the luminous panel can make the interior of a house seem more spacious. In this latter case, spill light from an adjoining room can be used rather than placing lamps in the panel. (The effect is not unlike that obtained with shoji screens.)

These panels are in many ways like luminous ceiling panels stood on end, but in the most important respect they are not. The illumination level of a luminous wall panel should not be high, unlike ceiling panels, because they must be viewed directly by persons in the room. Since walls are frequently darker than ceilings, intense luminosity can easily create a painfully bright glare.

The simplest way to achieve a softly glowing panel is to install a translucent panel of frosted glass or plastic in an interior wall, and to let lamps in another room provide the illumination. The technique will, of course, work only in interior walls, and will be efficient only if both rooms are usually used at the same time.

For an independently illuminated panel, there are two basic approaches. A tall vertical panel can be evenly lighted by a row of fluorescent or lumiline tubes down each of its sides. A long horizontal one can be lighted after the fashion of a cornice.

The depth of space behind the diffusing sheet largely determines the location of tubes within an enclosed space. In cases where the depth of space behind the diffusing material can exceed 6 inches, tubes can be mounted on the back surface near the corners. The resulting light will be even across the surface. The walls of the cavity will reflect most efficiently if they are painted a matte white.

In a shallower cavity, mounting tubes on the sides of the cavity near the diffusing panel may be a better solution, especially if studs interfere with the spreading of light across the back wall of the cavity. In such cases, tubes should be masked by an opaque (non-light-transmitting) trim to an angle of 45° to avoid bands of harsh light at each edge of the panel. In designing a translucent panel that will cross the faces of studs, allow a minimum clearance of two inches between the forward edges of the studs and the diffusing sheet to permit a maximum spread of light across the panel. Paint all inside surfaces in the cavity matte white.

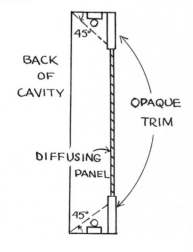

Most horizontal luminous panels are also the doors to storage space, either in the kitchen, or in a bedroom. Used in a way similar to the cornice, they help to create a feeling of spaciousness in a room that may otherwise lack windows and at the same time serve the useful function of lighting a closet or cupboard. Tubes are mounted close to the inside of the door panel, which may be of any translucent or transparent material, depending on the nature of the objects it contains. They are shielded from view by an opaque top trim deep enough to prevent someone using the closet or cupboard from seeing the light source when he looks into the top shelf of the storage space. The fixture channel should be mounted to leave enough clearance for easy lamp replacement, but should be at least even with the forward edge of shelving so the latter will not interfere with the spread of light to the lower part of the panel. As in all cases using reflected light, the interior of the cupboard should be painted matte white for the most efficient distribution of light. In cases where this solution is not practical because of other, decorative considerations, the palest coloration consistent with good taste is in order. In a china closet or a similarly formal furniture piece, transparent or translucent shelving can in part compensate for a lack of bright-colored surfaces.

CEILING LIGHT

While most wall lighting techniques depend on reflection, and a much narrower choice of direct lighting units exists, ceiling light turns the whole process about. It is in the main a matter of direct lighting, although in most cases reflection plays a part.

Cove

The notable exception to the general statement is cove lighting, an ancient technique currently in the midst of a revival. Cove lighting, probably the first type that comes to mind when you hear the words

"indirect light" is the reverse of the cornice. A projection from a wall contains the light source, which is directed entirely toward the ceiling. Unlike cornices, coves are used on all four walls, or on two opposite walls. A well-made cove provides enough light for navigation and for conversation, but it is a flat and even light that does not emphasize any decorative aspect in a room. For that reason it is almost always augmented by portable lamps or by some other decorative use of light. Reading or other critical-seeing tasks also require a supporting light.

If light is to spread evenly across a ceiling, the distance from tube to ceiling should be a minimum of 12 inches. Even greater distance is more efficient.

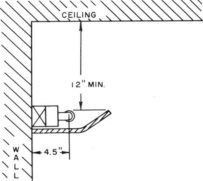

The distance from long axis of the tube to wall should be no less than 4½ inches to prevent excessive wall brightness. The wall and ceiling should be of a matte finish, in the 65-85% reflectance range. (Swirled plaster finishes do not work well because the reflected shadow patterns look like soiled patches on the ceiling.) The inside of the cove trough, as usual, functions best if it is matte white.

The lip of the trough controls the spread of light from a cove, and it shields the tubes from view. If the lip is too low, the tubes may be visible from the far wall of the room. If it is too high, the light will be restricted to a narrow area above the cove. To determine how high the lip should be, draw a line from a point

68 inches above the floor at the far wall to the top of the proposed location of the tube. Draw a second line from the intersection of the ceiling

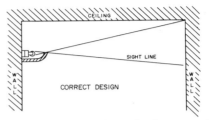

with the far wall to the bottom of the tube. The inside edge of the cove's lip should fall at the point of intersection of these two lines. (Draw the diagram to scale on engineer's paper.) You can often add cove lighting to the tops of cabinets that are above eye-level. The same considerations apply.

Soffits and troffers

Soffit or troffer lighting is diffused and recessed light placed in the underside of an architectural member. The distinction between soffit and troffer is sometimes thin, but the soffit light is generally a unit not in the main ceiling while the troffer is. The soffit light may be in a section of dropped ceiling. It may be combined with a cove for a part of the cove's length. It may be shelved out over a dressing table mirror.

The soffit is usually built in scale with a sofa, or with some work surface to provide even illumination over the entire object it lights. There are pre-wired manufactured units available in a fairly wide range of sizes. The typical ones have nominal widths of 1 foot or 2 feet, and nominal lengths equal to a variety of fluorescent tube sizes, or multiples of them. They come with a reflecting shield. Variations in the assembly are designed to make installation in differing types of ceiling as easy as possible. Depths of these manufactured fixtures vary. Two standard depths are 4⅞ inches and 5⅞ inches, each of which will fit into a ceiling plenum between 2x8 rafters. Some extremely shallow units are on the market for lesser plenums.

The troffer, not always so closely tied to a single object as is the soffit, usually is one of these manufactured units. In some cases you may find it necessary to fashion your own unit.

A narrow soffit or troffer, using only one row of tubes, should be 6 to 8 inches deep and no more than 20 inches wide. Tubes will not appear as streaks on the diffusing panel (plastic or glass) if they are 6 inches above it. The entire cavity should be painted flat white, including any pipes that may run through the space. If you recess a home-built soffit or troffer between rafters, it may be more efficient if you block the ends of the cavity with reflecting material. Wood painted white is adequate. If you do this, always leave some open space for ventilation.

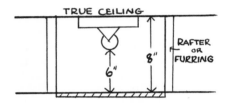

Rows of incandescent bulbs (60-watt, spaced 2 feet on centers) can be used in place of fluorescent tubes.

The combined cove-and-soffit is different from regular soffits in that it has no reflecting surface above the light sources, whether they are incandescent or fluorescent. This means that the intensity of down-light through the diffusing panels is less than that obtained from pure soffits or troffers. However, light reflecting from the wall and ceiling above the unit spreads farther and

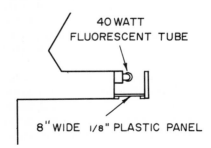

more evenly. In designing such a light source, keep in mind that the rules for coves take precedence since the cove can be a greater potential source of glare.

If your situation is not readily adaptable to lines of light, recessed or semi-recessed incandescent units with glass or plastic diffusing shields are made in a number of small rectangles or squares, usually in the range of 10 to 18 inches diameter (diagonal). Some of them are especially designed to fit in shallow cavities. Others are made so they can be extended down from a ceiling slightly without producing glare spots (the diffusing shield is curved to fit flush with the ceiling; a deep shadow between ceiling line and the edge of the bright face of the fixture is a source of glare).

Luminous Panels and Ceilings

The luminous ceiling, covering either the entire ceiling surface, or a large part of it, is an efficient way to light many areas in the home, and can be rather easy to install. The fully luminous ceiling usually is found in kitchens and baths, where glare-free and shadow-free light is important to cooking or to shaving and makeup. As diffusing materials have become more versatile and decorative, and as dimmers have become more efficient, luminous ceilings and panels have found acceptance in living and dining rooms, and in entry halls.

The luminous ceiling is the fullest expression of the broad-source lighting technique in popular use today. The underlying principle is a large-size, low-brightness source that can be viewed directly with comfort, but which lights a room or a part of a room from all directions through diffusion and reflection of light generated by a source. In this connection of luminous ceilings, low-brightness is a relative expression. In living room or dining room use, the brightness should be low indeed, because persons sitting in conversation in an extended area will

usually see some of the ceiling at the far wall. If it is too much brighter than walls or furnishings, the contrast may be irritating. Also, the even, shadow-free light tends to reduce the feeling of volume (three dimensional effect), which depends to a degree on shadows. Without this, a room tends to be uninteresting. In kitchens the amount of light generated should be rather high, usually about twice as high as in living rooms. The ceiling is usually smaller in area, so not as visible. The general surroundings are often lighter in color, so contrast may not be as great a problem. And the work in the kitchen requires close seeing on a plane about 30 inches off the floor (counter height), so light intensity from the source needs to be strong.

The differences in level can be achieved in a number of ways, used in combinations or separately. Possible means are: The number of tubes or bulbs and their size, the nature of the cavity in which they are enclosed, the nature of the diffusing material, and the relative amount of the ceiling made luminous. (In living rooms it often amounts to as little as 25% of the total ceiling surface. In kitchens the average range is much higher.)

There are two basic types of ready-to-install luminous ceilings on the market. One is the floating luminous panel or ceiling, which hangs from the original ceiling of the house. The light channels are mounted on a standard outlet box in the ceiling. Chains hold a lightweight aluminum frame to the channel. Plastic diffusing panels are then laid into the aluminum frame, and the installation is complete.

Single units are 4x5 feet, and employ two 40-watt fluorescent tubes. Prices range from about $65 to slightly more than $100 per unit.

These floating panels occupy a space 7½ inches deep if the outlet box is mounted in the ceiling. (The National Building Code requires that ceilings be no less than 7½ feet from the floor, which may preclude your using this type of unit if your ceilings are already near the minimum.) However, in a room with extremely high ceilings, the units can be dropped to any distance by means of jointed metal poles or other devices to extend wiring from the ceiling downward. This application must be designed with care to avoid glare if the panel does not fill a space fully. The dark area around and above the panel may not be filled in by light escaping up from the tubes used with the panel unit. The loss of light caused by lack of a proper reflecting surface can help to reduce the surface brightness if that is desirable, or can be avoided by fashioning a suitable reflector. Gypsum board painted white and fastened 7 inches above the diffusing panels will serve in place of an ordinary ceiling painted white. (Darker paints in the cavity can also help to reduce excessive brightness.)

The other "kit" on the market is only slightly more complex to install. It uses a system of "tees and brackets" to support plastic panels. The entire installation (not considering the wiring) can be done with a few hand tools. This assembly can be adapted to fit any ceiling area. The basic panel sizes are 2x2 and 2x4 feet, but both panels and supporting members can be cut to fit. These ceilings require more planning than the free-floating panels. The distance from the ceiling to the panels is left to you, as is the spacing of tubes in the cavity created by adding the ceiling.

Manufacturers recommend, in general, that the distance from panel surface to tube equal one-half the distance between tubes for even brightness. They also recommend that tubes be a minimum of 7 inches from the diffusing panels.

The depth of the cavity, if you follow these general recommendations, will do much to determine the brightness level of the ceiling. The deeper the cavity, the less light will reach the panels, and the fewer tubes you will need to achieve an even brightness level. One manufacturer recommends one 40-watt fixture per 15 square feet for medium brightness (living rooms), one 40-watt fixture for each 10 square feet for high light (kitchens, baths), and one 40-watt fixture per 7 square feet for extra high light (also kitchens, work rooms).

These units also use lightweight aluminum frames. Long channels are secured to each wall at the desired height of the finished ceiling. Snap-in tabs secure main tees (cross-bars) to these wall units, and the same type tabs secure shorter cross tees to main tees. (Straps attached to the original ceiling provide additional support.)

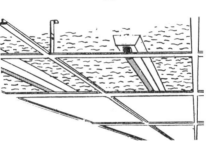

As with all other broad-source lighting techniques, the reflecting surfaces in the cavity are of prime importance. For maximum efficiency, sheet foil can be used. Flat white paint is nearly as effective, and less troublesome to deal with. All fixture mountings, exposed pipes, or other objects in the cavity will appear as dark streaks unless they too are painted white.

The basic approaches of the manufactured units will serve well for custom units you might wish to design for yourself.

There are two other approaches to the luminous ceiling, each posing some special problems.

The first is the use of fluorescent tubes or incandescent bulbs mounted in the spaces between joists or rafters. To obtain even light, you will need to mount a fixture on each side of each rafter or joist. Mounting them on one side only will cause some shadow near the opposite joist even if panels are suspended well below the joists on some type of metal or wood framework. This difficulty can be partly overcome by using relatively wide lath or other supporting strips to hold the panels. In this case, the grid layout should be designed to match the joist or rafter system. The photo on page 29 is an example of this approach, which may be the only one possible in low-ceilinged houses.

Another way to achieve low brightness levels is the use of long rows of small-wattage incandescent bulbs above each side of a panel. The sketch below is the construction detail from the photo on page 18.

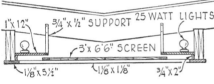

Skylights

A considerable number of the luminous ceiling panels shown in the photographic chapters are combined with skylights. The combination is a natural one, because the light coming from such units is similar in daytime or at night. There are several ways to get artificial light into a skylight. Before describing them, however, some general information on skylights might be of help.

There are some practical points to consider before locating a skylight.

1. Unshaded outside light from above is brighter than reflected light entering through vertical windows. You might get all the light you want through the smallest available pre-fabricated skylight (about 14 inches square).

2. Daylight also means sun heat. Any skylight will add some heat to a room. This is extremely important

to remember when dealing with a windowless room or one with an existing heat problem. You will probably want to consider the kinds of skylights that can reflect much of the heat and still permit some light to enter. Or you may be able to tilt the skylight until it receives only north light (or place it on a roof pitched toward the north).

3. Moisture tends to condense on skylights, especially when there is a wide difference between outside and inside temperature. Dripping from the inside is especially a problem in the Northern states and in mountain areas. Since moisture that collects at the corners may eventually weaken the frame, most prefabricated skylights have condensation gutters.

Most prefabricated skylight domes are designed for the addition of a dome-shaped second layer of plastic below the outside dome. Adding this inner dome creates an insulating air space between the two layers, which prevents condensation and also helps to diffuse the light. A similar function is performed by a flat plate of plastic or glass placed flush with the ceiling at the bottom of a light well.

A single unshielded bulb can be mounted well up inside one of these dome units with a curved piece of conduit serving as the support and as protection for wiring.

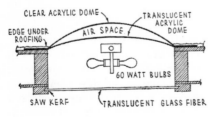

If the structure of the ceiling permits, bulbs can also be set in the cavity on either side. In either case, a shield of diffusing plastic at finished ceiling level will hide the presence of bulbs during the day (the farther they are from the plas-

tic panel, the less chance there is of their casting any shadow).

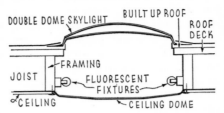

In skylight combinations, the PAR-type flood or spotlight is often the best solution where there is a deep cavity, especially if the skylight is not an insulating type. The hard glass bulbs can withstand moisture and cold.

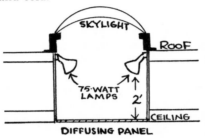

If you have attic space, the combination skylight-luminous ceiling panel will work better if you fashion a light well around the openings in the attic space. The material should be of white matte finish for maximum efficiency. If the ceiling panel lifts out easily, such a unit can provide a handy means of getting into the attic if one side of the light well is used as a door that can be swung back when needed. Your approach to fashioning a light well will depend entirely on the nature of the crawl space.

Diffusing agents

Glass and plastic continue as the two commonest diffusing agents for ceiling-mounted lights, with metal louvers and egg-crates a third possibility.

Glass can be made to diffuse in two different ways, by coating it with "frost," or by molding it so it acts as a lens. The frosted glass technique works in much the same way

as translucent plastics. The lens approach is another story altogether. The glass is molded with ridges and hollows at precise angles so that light is directed within narrow limits. The result is that you don't see a sharp glare as you look toward the fixture (usually a semi-recessed ceiling unit), even though light is being beamed out at a number of angles. The technique spreads light evenly over a larger area than it would cover if left to its own nature. Commonest types are fresnel lens (broad spread) and asymmetric (directional control).

Plastic diffusing panels vary enormously in their transmitting qualities according to the thickness of the sheet, the type of plastic used, tinting, and the presence or absence of louvers or "light cells" in the core. Some of the improved acrylic plastics resist discoloration under sunlight (older formulae tended to yellow with exposure), making them ideal for use in skylights (or with fluorescent tubes, which emit some ultra-violet light).

Light transmittance of various panels commonly used in lighting ranges from considerably less than 45% (the most-used type) to more 65%.

Some specially manufactured types contain louvers to direct light. onto a wall for decorative purposes, or onto the face of a person using a mirror for shaving or makeup.

The main advantage of plastic over glass as a diffusing agent is its extreme light weight. Sheets weigh from 3 to 10 ounces per square foot in common thicknesses. Also, there is a greater control over the finish surface. Plastic can be washed simply by soaking it in a mild detergent solution. (Manufacturers advise that sheets should never be rubbed, either during washing or drying. They retain finish longer, maintain anti-static properties better.) Chemical cleaning compounds are often injurious, especially to panels with any decorative tints. (To minimize washing, use panels so no open spaces are around them to let in dust, insects.)

The metal egg-crate louvers are a common diffusing agent of a somewhat different type. They screen direct view of the light source to an angle of 45° (the angle at which you no longer see the fixture without looking up), and serve as reflecting devices to spread the light. The most usual type used for large areas is the square grid, but circular variations are often found on ceiling-recessed or ceiling-mounted cone lamps designed to provide strong light on a work surface.

A recent contribution in this vein is the honeycomb plastic panel, which uses tiny openings in a thin shield rather than large ones in a thicker shield.

PORTABLE LAMPS

Increasing emphasis on design of portable and ceiling or wall-mounted light fixtures has made something of a mockery of the old "proper" proportions for lamps of the type. A wealth of new shielding materials allows better control of the spread of light than the traditional cylindrical shade for some purposes (the latter still has its place).

There are only a few general points to consider in choosing lamps of these types.

The spread of light should be in scale with the purpose for which the light is used. Reading lamps, for example, should spread a fairly large pool of light because the book occupies but a small part of the field of vision as you read. A bright light on its pages but not beyond will produce painful contrast in most cases. Hooded lamps, commonly used by draughtsmen, should be supplemented by a large overhead source for the same reason, although their concentrated beam is useful in the specific task.

If used as general light, these fixtures should cast light both up and down. A lamp with a solid shade

(opaque) above the bulb will create a sharp contrast in light level reflected from the wall below it as compared to the wall above.

Similarly, the shield should be in a rough balance with its background. A floor lamp with a highly transmitting shade against a dark wood wall can be painfully bright. A ceiling-mounted fixture with too bright a diffusing bowl can produce the same effect.

These difficulties can be offset if lamps used for local lighting have their faults offset by other sources of general light.

A number of fanciful fixtures for decorative lighting purposes fall beyond the scope of any "rules." Their low-wattage bulbs are not hard on the eyes unless they are set against an extremely dark background. (note the examples on page 21).

SWITCHES AND DIMMERS

Light switches come today in many forms. The old toggle switch that you flipped on and off with a click, or groped for in the dark, has given way to an impressive variety of switches with special features.

A good many switches don't click. Most are pushed rather than flipped. Some glow softly so you can find them at night, or they light up brightly to tell you something is left on, or they dim the lighting to suit the occasion, or they stay on for a minute after you turn them off, or they go on automatically at nightfall.

The variety available seems confusing but it is really quite practical. One or another of these switches may prove a great convenience for controlling some of the lights in your home, and they are an inexpensive luxury. All the ones we list here are 115-volt switches. They can simply replace existing switches in your home, requiring no costly change in wiring, as would special circuits or a low voltage system. Even the dimmers, formerly big and expensive, have been considerably reduced in

price and made so compact they fit in ordinary switch boxes. As each of these switches has its own unique purpose, we describe each type separately here.

Feather-touch. This type of switch does nothing new, but does the old job better. You barely touch the top of its rocker-arm and it goes on, touch the bottom and it goes off. It is very quiet, and compact enough so a pair can be mounted on a single plate.

The type costs about $2 each and you will probably find it only at electrical supply stores, whereas you can buy an ordinary toggle switch for about 35 cents at a variety store. But the ordinary toggle switch has a fast-wearing knife-blade contact inside it, while the contacts in this new switch are long-wearing silver points (similar to the distributor points in your car) that are specially designed for alternating current. You almost never have to replace one.

Push-button. You push these switches to turn lights on, again to turn them off. Standard toggle-switch plates fit over them. The buttons on some of these glow softly when the switch is off (they contain tiny neon tubes). You can find the glowing buttons easily in the dark and they also serve as minute night-lights to guide you around a dark room. Some other models have much brighter indicator lights inside the buttons, usually red, that light up when the switch is on. These remind you that the driveway flood light has been left on.

These switches also have long-wearing "A-C points." Different makes vary from less than a dollar to $2.25 (the latter are "lifetime"). You find them at electrical supply houses and hardware stores.

Weatherproofed. With the advent of the push-button switches, you no longer need to weatherproof a switch on the exterior of the house with an unattractive metal cover containing a lever. This heavy neoprene rubber cover simply fits over the switch and its box, sealing it from dampness. You push its flexible center to operate the switch. The cost is around $2.50.

Roundbutton and flat plate. These two are decorative switches. The cover plate of the button type and the activator plate of the flat type are available in clear plastic so you can back them with wallpaper, paint, or fabric to match that of the room. You tap the flat plate anywhere near its top to turn the switch on, near the bottom to turn it off. You just push the round button anywhere to turn it on or off. Both types cost about $2 each. Both also contain long-wearing "A-C points."

Combination type. This compact type of switch is not new but has been greatly improved lately. It allows up to three switches (or combinations of three with outlets and indicator lights, as shown in photo) in a single switch box. The outlets are grounded. You press one side of the quiet rocker-arm switch to turn it on and the other to turn it off. The rocker-arm is luminous to be seen in the dark. Cost is 85 cents per switch.

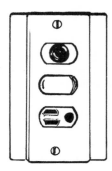

Mercury toggle. Mercury switches are also not new but this latest version (like some push-buttons) has a tiny neon locator light in its toggle that glows whenever the switch is off. Mercury switches have been very popular for over a decade because they make contact by joining two tiny pools of mercury and therefore are completely silent. They are long-

lasting under the average lighting load. However they seldom stand up as well as the newer mechanical switches under a heavy load. Cost with locator light is about $1.75.

Delay toggle. This switch looks like any ordinary toggle switch but it introduces to the United States the old European idea of "la minuterie." That is, it does not turn off the lights right when you flip it, but turns them off about a minute later, giving you time to walk instead of grope to the bed after turning off the bedroom lights, or time to saunter (but without detours) out to the car after turning off the entryway lights. Cost is about $3.

Photo-electric. Costing about $14, this switch automatically turns lights on at dusk and turns them off at dawn. It can replace an ordinary switch on the exterior of your home, or be placed anywhere on the exterior or on an interior wall facing a window area. A light-duty switch, its capacity is about 300 watts (about a fifth that of most wall switches), but this is usually ample for residential lighting.

It is often used to light up a garden or entryway automatically at nightfall. It can also be used to turn on a bedroom's lights at night when you are away, thus making a prowler think the house is occupied. For this use, an ordinary switch is included to make the circuit inoperative at other times.

Dimmers

An increasing variety of dimmers is now available, largely due to the adaptation of devices originally intended to miniaturize electronics equipment. Almost all of them have very specific capacities, and should be bought with their limitations in mind.

Push-button dimmer. This is one of the new full-range electronic dimmers. You turn the knob like a radio's volume control to vary a room's illumination to anything from zero to full brightness. With

this version, you just push the knob to turn the lights off or on, and thus do not need to change its dimness setting. Its capacity is 600 watts (incandescent lamps only). The cover plate is the decorative type and comes with an extra clear plastic insert. Cost is $15.

Any full-range dimmer is excellent for controlling the amount of illumination in your living room, dining room, or garden, and for leaving lights just barely glowing throughout the night in the nursery or bathroom. Like theatrical lighting, it smoothly changes the illumination to suit your need or mood.

T-F dimmer. This is another of the full-range 600-watt electronic dimmers. It can be used to control either incandescent or fluorescent lamps, or both.

On fluorescent, it will control some types of ballast boxes, but not others. Check with a dealer if you already have fluorescent light units installed and wish to add a dimmer control. Like the push-button, you operate this dimmer like a radio volume control, but you turn the knob fully counterclockwise to switch the lights off. The cost is about $33 (an incandescent-only model costs about $15).

High-low dimmer. This is one of the low-cost electronic dimmers. It sells for $5. The toggle switch has three positions: Up for full brightness, center for off, and down for dim (about 40% of full brightness). Its capacity is 300 watts.

All three of these dimmers can replace ordinary switches as they will fit inside standard switch boxes. They should not be used to control any appliance; they are made for lighting only. Neither should dimmers be used with portable lamps; the cords are not heavy enough.

These dimmers work on a different principle from that of a rheostat, auto-transformer, or saturable reactor type of control. Their circuits vary somewhat but are essentially the same principle: Assemblies of silicon switches or rectifiers, potentiometers, resistors, and condensers change or block off a portion of each cycle of the alternating current that is flowing to the lamps. The important thing is that they themselves use only a small percentage of the current when dimming a light, therefore give off little heat, and therefore can be small enough to go in a standard switch box.

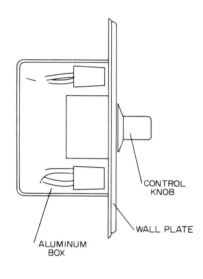

CONTROL KNOB

WALL PLATE

ALUMINUM BOX

When you dim lights with these, you are saving electricity (not wasting it as heat in the control), and light bulbs operating on low intensity last many times longer.

As a general practice, whatever type of dimmer you may use, you may find it wise to "season" lamps, especially fluorescent tubes, for as many burning hours as possible up to 100 before dimming them. This also will add to their life span.

Low-voltage switching

Low-voltage switching, as the name states, does not use regular house current to operate switches. Not practical in most remodels, it has advantages worth considering in new construction, or in additions where you would not have to tear off wall surfaces to run wiring.

A system of relays, transformers, and (in complex circuits) rectifiers, permits the use of small wires using 24 volts (well below the threshhold of painful shock) between a fixture and the switch that controls it. This

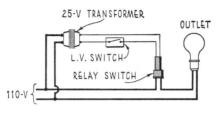

25-V TRANSFORMER

OUTLET

L.V. SWITCH

RELAY SWITCH

110-V

low-voltage wire is less expensive than heavy-duty types for normal use, and also reduces the voltage drain customary in ordinary switches by shortening the length of regular wiring runs. The system can be used for single switches, although it is most commonly used in a master system for remote control. In these master systems, all lights in the house can be controlled from a single point, the master bedroom for example, as well as individually. The low-voltage switch also combines the functions of single pole and three-way switches (so a single fixture can be controlled from different points, as in the case of stair or hall lights).

Typical face plates look like those of standard switches. Master control units are also compact, and have a separate on-off switch mounted with the selector to engage or disengage the master control from the branch circuits.

WIRING AND CIRCUITS

Electricity, like a pet lion, must be treated with all due respect, or it will bite. Understanding the habits of this enormously useful servant—electricity, not the lion—is the best safeguard against being bitten. The thing is not to get overly intimate with electricity unless you are trained to work with it. But there is a great deal the average homeowner

can and should know about it, whether he is remodeling his wiring system or simply trying to get the maximum safe use from an existing system.

According to Webster, electricity is a fundamental quality of nature. When it moves in a stream, it gives rise to a magnetic field of force associated with kinetic energy. What this means, simply, is that electric current introduced through wires into a machine will cause the machine to do work, whether the machine is a light bulb, refrigerator, or a saw motor. This field of force is measured in the familiar terms, volts and amperes. The kinetic energy is measured in watts.

Electricity moves along a wire much as water flows through a pipe. It is pushed by a pressure measured in volts. The amount of current, the flow, is measured in amperes, a word which expresses both amount and time interval, like gallons per minute when you speak of water. Pressure and current together produce power, the direct equivalent of horsepower. Electrically, such power is measured in watts. The three brought together form this useful equation:

Volts x amperes = watts.

This formula is the basis of all design of electrical circuits in the modern home. If you live in a community where the power is regulated at 115-230v, the circuits that carry your lights and small appliances will probably be fused at 15 or 20 amperes. Applying the equation above, a 110v, 15 ampere circuit will safely yield 1,650 watts of power. A 20 ampere circuit carries a potential of 2,200 watts. Circuits of this type are called branch circuits. There may be other, heavier circuits for major appliances. These are usually 200v, 60 (or more) ampere, and serve electric ranges, laundry appliances and heavy-duty tools in work shops.

A typical post-war home of moderate size will have six to twelve branch circuits. A small apartment may have as few as two. A large home may have as many as twenty. Pre-war homes, especially those built in the 1920s, will have only a few simple circuits unless the wiring has been renovated. The kinds of equipment and materials used in electrical systems of different eras will vary considerably. Technical improvements have come at an ever increasing rate over the past few years. In many cases you can decide just about how old your wiring is by examining some of its elements.

From the utility pole to the little lamp in the bedroom, electricity uses a bewildering complex of equipment to get its job done. The elements all connect to one another by wires of various types. Each of the elements must match the others in its circuit in capacity. And the system has to be coherent as a whole. It is here that most amateur electricians go astray, and it is for this reason that many municipal codes forbid "bootleg" wiring jobs, and that many insurance companies look dimly upon fire claims filed by homeowners who circumvented code provisions. It is for this reason that this book makes no effort to explain how to make any type of electrical connection. The subject is a vast one. One "simplified" wiring manual runs to somewhat more than 600 pages. A professional electrician is in order for any major wiring job.

Service entry: The utility company brings electricity to the wall of your home, passes it through a

meter, and terminates its wires at the service entry. It provides both 115 volts and 230 volts service, unless you have no heavy appliances calling for the heavier line.

The service entry is what most of us call the "fuse box."

Variations: In some older homes you may find meter, main disconnect switch, and fuses more widely separated. Newer, larger, or more expensive homes may have meter and main disconnect switch outside and a circuit breaker on a wall inside the house.

Main disconnect switch: In the service entry described above, you shut off the electricity by pulling out two insulating blocks from the panel inside the metal box. "Range" shuts off only the electric range. "Main" controls the rest of the house. When a block is pulled out it looks like this:

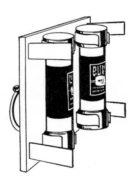

On the back of each block are cartridge-type fuses which protect the wiring in the box from any damage in case there should be a sudden upsurge of current in the entrance wire. "Main" has 60-ampere fuses. "Range" has "non-50" fuses. (A fuse labeled "non" or "one-time" is non-renewable. It costs less than a dollar in this size. If it blows out, you throw it away. The other type has replaceable metal strips. It is originally more expensive.

Variations: The main disconnect on many houses is a throw switch with blades operated by a handle.

Another type is built into a metal cabinet in such a way that you kill the circuit when you open the cabinet door.

The fuses on the main line coming into the house may be any one of these three types:

It is a general rule in most communities that you can use two 30 ampere plug fuses (as large as they come) on the main line if you have no more than two circuits branching off into the house.

In a house that has no more than six branch circuits, an installation without a main disconnect switch, main fuses, and all other fuses is allowed when you use a circuit breaker.

Each circuit is controlled by a separate switch. An overload opens the circuit and throws the switch to the "off" position. To close the circuit again, move the switch to "reset" then let it fall back to "on."

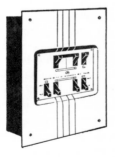

The circuit breaker eliminates fuses, affords protection, and permits temporary overloads that would blow ordinary fuses.

Branch circuit fuses: A typical house might have six branch circuits, controlled by six plug fuses on the panel at the service entrance—three 20 ampere (red), two 15 ampere (blue), and one 6¼ ampere (brown). Older fuses were interchangeable; the entrance capacity of a circuit could be changed simply by installing a larger fuse. The newer "fusestat" avoids this potential danger. An adapter ring is permanently locked into each fuse receptacle. It will accept only the size

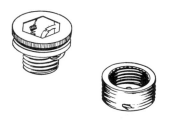

fuse for which the circuit was designed. Thus there is no danger of putting a 30 ampere fuse on a circuit which has a maximum safe capacity of 20 amperes, for example.

Variations: Some homes will have as few as two circuits, others will have a dozen or more. The plug fuse is still the most widely used type. One plug fuse now available is a time-lag type. It permits a temporary overload on circuits which service appliances with motors, which often has to overcome a heavy initial resistance before it settles down to normal operation. (Heaters can also fall into this category.)

The National Electrical Code, supplemented by local codes, specifies a fuse of a certain amperage to match the size of wire used in the circuit. The size of the wire determines how much electric current will pass through, just as the size of pipe limits the flow of water. If you give a wire more current than it should carry, you waste power. In the extreme case resistance will heat the wire to the ignition point, raising the possibility of fire. Most house circuits have No. 14 wire (or larger) for easy flow of 15 ampere current. The usual plug circuit has a 20 ampere fuse, requiring No. 12

wire or larger. If you find larger fuses on a branch circuit, you might be wise to have an electrician check the whole circuit.

Testing circuits

It is always handy to know which light fixtures, appliances, or convenience outlets are on which branch circuit. It is especially handy if you are planning to remodel, or to add new light fixtures in the home. If you know what the capacity of the circuit is, and what its current operating load is, you can better decide where to add new appliances or fixtures. If you are adding rooms, you can often save time and money by realizing what effect a change of use in presently existing rooms will have on your wiring system.

It is not difficult to trace out branch circuits. The first step, if you have plug fuses, is to throw the main disconnect switch. Remove one branch circuit fuse, and return the main disconnect to "on." Then go to each switch and see if it works. For convenience outlets not in current use, carry a small lamp and plug it into each one. Repeat the process for each branch circuit, keeping a chart of outlets it serves. (You might want to paste the chart near the service entry for convenient reference). Total up the number of watts being drawn on the circuit, and match that figure with its capacity. If you are going to remodel, you will have a rough idea of how much added wiring you will need, and of how much reserve you have in certain areas of the house. (You may find your circuits "overloaded" in some cases. Your fuses will be safe as long as you don't turn everything on at once.)

The proliferation of portable appliances of all types—high fidelity phonographs, hair dryers, movie projectors—has at last led to one basic change in home wiring. There are more convenience outlets, and more specialization of them.

The old convenience outlet, or wall

plug, simply had two wires for alternating current. You stuck a plug into it and that was that. As long as portable lamps and small radios were all they served, they were adequate. Now, however, many appliances (especially in the kitchen) require grounding. Many homes have 3-prong outlets for the purpose. Other appliances work best if they match pole-for-pole the current supply. Their plugs have one prong larger than the other, and will fit only in outlets built to receive them. Neither type of convenience outlet affects old-style plugs, which still are used on portable lamps.

The lack of convenience outlets for appliances can in part be compensated for by raceways. These are in effect extensions of a single convenience outlet. Some of them can be plugged into it. Others must be spliced into the outlet box itself. None of them will increase the amount of current available. They only offer more places to plug appliances into existing current supplies. Most of them are rated at 15 amperes, and will accommodate kitchen appliances such as beaters and blenders, or radio or phonograph sets. Cost ranges from 20 cents a foot to about $2 a foot. You might investigate the several types on the market to see which is best suited to your needs.

OUTDOOR WIRING

Outdoor wiring requires some special handling because it is exposed to weather, and because it does not have the protective armor of house walls to keep it out of harm's way.

The system, depending on the amount of living you do outdoors, can range from a simple temporary set-up to an elaborate scheme that approaches the indoor wiring in complexity. Many outdoor circuits must be standard 115-volt lines to light utility areas, porches and the like. Garden and patio lighting may be either standard circuits or special low-voltage circuits. The former can be quite expensive. The latter are a good deal less costly.

Few homes have surplus capacity enough to add outdoor lighting systems without increasing the number of branch circuits. If this is the case, your service entry will have to be rewired to include the additional load. In some cases, entry wires from the service pole may need to be augmented. Each of these is an expensive operation, and must be done by a professional electrician.

Because of the expense, plans for a new outdoor circuit (or circuits) should be drawn with considerable care to avoid the sort of oversights that leave you cursing the darkness rather than enjoying the candle after the work is done. The best approach is to draw a scale plan of the grounds, and to note on it the types of light you wish, and the locations in which units will be placed. With these factors in mind, you will be in a better position to work out efficient routes for stringing or burying cable. Don't overlook outdoor outlets for electric tools such as hedge trimmers, lawn mowers and the like. These outlets are also convenient for adding lights for a party, or Christmas decorations.

Permanent circuits
More expensive than other types of outdoor wiring, and harder to move around than the others, they offer a greater potential. They can be adapted to more purposes, and are always ready. Temporary hookups or low-voltage systems lack one quality or the other.

All elements of an outdoor circuit should be purchased and installed with durability in mind. Municipal codes are unfailingly strict about the materials used. All outlets, switches, splice boxes, lamp sockets and wires must be of approved weatherproof types. (Rainy days and damp nights are conducive to short circuiting in improperly sealed connections.)

Outdoor cable must be either the direct-burial neoprene type, or must be sheathed in rigid conduit if it is run underground. No. 14 cable is required on 15 ampere circuits with runs of 100 feet or less. No. 12 wire is used for longer runs or for circuits of higher amperage.

Either type of cable should be buried in a trench one shovel blade wide and 18 to 24 inches deep as a protection against accidental severing by a shovel or other sharp instrument. If the trench must be shallower, the cable or conduit can be fastened with brackets to the underside of 1x3 or 1x4 redwood strips as a substitute protective device.

At any point where the cable leaves the ground, it must be protected either by rigid conduit, or by flexible conduit secured to a wooden post. In some instances, the cable can be secured to a fence or screen post to serve this purpose.

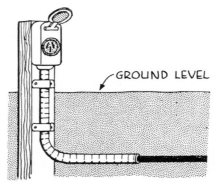

Sometimes it is desirable or necessary to run cable overhead. Most municipal codes require that overhead cable be sheathed in rigid conduit if it is 8 feet or less above the ground. Higher runs can be left exposed if they are passed through strain insulators (like those on utility pole cross-arms) at intervals of 15 feet. If the cable follows the trunk of a tree, you may find it wise to save wear and tear on the insulation by encasing it in thin-wall tubing. The same measure is often

taken if cable runs along a patio overhead as a safety precaution.

Any length of cable which enters a switch, outlet, or splice box from above should be strung with a drip loop is prevent water from seeping through the punch-out around the cable, and causing a short circuit in the box.

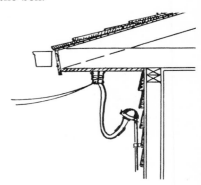

You may be able to do much of the groundwork for a system of this type yourself, but all terminal connections should be made by a licensed electrician. Most municipalities require that the system be inspected before any of its cables are covered. Call for an inspection as soon as the electrician is finished to avoid any later difficulties with code requirements.

In purchasing light fixtures for a permanent system, or in making your own, be sure to get weather-resistant materials. Sun, wind and rain all take their toll. The common materials are aluminum, brass, copper and stainless steel among metals, and hard-finish plastics and ceramic materials.

If you use PAR lamps, they can be left exposed to the weather, but all the "soft" glass bulbs need additional protection. Fairly high wattage bulbs, especially if within range of sprinklers, can be placed in vapor-proof shields. The precaution is not necessary, but can help to prolong the life of bulbs. Fluorescent tubes can be used outdoors in special water-tight housing (see photo on page 72).

Some of the basic outdoor lamp

types are shown in the sketch below.

It is not a bad idea, although not required, to use grounds on all outdoor outlets and switches. Buried conduit is an automatic ground. Other solutions may need a copper wire running into the soil from the outlet. In purchasing new outlets, you may want to consider getting the grounded, three-hole type. Some garden tools are now equipped with the three-prong plugs as a safety factor.

Temporary Installations

The minimal temporary lighting system can be no more than an approved 3-wire (grounded) weatherproof extension cord plugged into an indoor convenience outlet and run through an open window. Most use extension cords plugged into one or more outlets on a house wall or near it. Systems of this type are not especially practical for garden lighting, but they can serve well for patio parties.

In using any extension cord outdoors, for any purpose, make all connections to it before you connect it to a live circuit. Short circuits happen all too easily when a cord has been in damp grass. Making connections to a "live" cord can be fatal if a short does occur while you are standing in a wet area.

If you have no outdoor outlets, in some cases it is possible to tap off an indoor outlet without great difficulty. If the indoor circuit can take an added load, wires can be led through punchouts in the back of an existing box, through the wall, and out to another box outdoors. Be sure the regular circuit is capable of handling whatever loads may be imposed as a result of the added outlet.

Low-voltage systems

The low-voltage garden light is an inexpensive and attractive alternative to standard circuits. It is mobile even after installation, and provides brighter light than its 6 to 12-volt power might indicate (automobile lights are 12 volt systems). There is no danger of uncomfortable shock with these systems.

The standard kit contains 100 feet of plastic-covered cable and 6 light units, which operate off a transformer. The transformer can handle an additional 6 lights (and a total of 200 feet of cable). These can be bought separately, as can inexpensive connectors which permit the setting up of spur lines. A grounded 3-prong adapter can be purchased so transformer can be plugged into standard 2-hole outlets if you have none of the grounded type. The transformer must be shielded from the weather.

The earliest kits had only cone shields for the lamps. Later types offer a variety of lamp housings, including mushroom types. Lamps are attached to cable by slitting cable, pressing lamp base tightly against it.

The cable need be buried only an inch or two beneath soil, but its path should be marked to avoid accidental severing with garden tool.

Gaslight

Gaslights in either closed or open flame units are cheerful and efficient outdoor lights for entryways or patios.

The typical entry light is a "post" lantern harking back to the day of the carriage and footman. This type can also be used well on patios, where its yellow light does not attract night insects. The open-flame "luau torch" is another possibility.

Installation is, of course, to be done by the utility company.

There are two types of mantle lights (that is, controlled flame), the inverted mantle and the upright. Industry studies show the inverted mantle to be the brighter and evener light. But it is also the hardest to operate. Either type is long-lived and relatively inexpensive to operate. Side panes in these posts should have some diffusing qualities to minimize glare in the eyes of persons using walks near them.

Insect lights

One of the most difficult problems to deal with in lighted outdoor areas at night is an excess insect population. Insects are strongly attracted by light in the blue range of the spectrum, and only slightly attracted by light in the yellow range. There are, aside from placing lights as far away from doorways or patios as possible, several insect traps on the market to help. These are equipped with a blue light to lure insects to the trap, which kills them either chemically or electrically. A simpler device is the blue decoy light placed away from inhabited areas.

EQUIPMENT MANUFACTURERS

The quickest and easiest way to get specific product information is a visit to a local retail electric shop or hardware store. If you are unable to find a specific product, the following partial list of manufacturers will be able to provide you with information and a nearby retail outlet.

LAMPS

Large Lamp Dept.
General Electric Co.
Nela Park
Cleveland 12, Ohio

Sylvania Lighting Products Co.
60 Boston St.
Salem, Mass.

Lamp Division
Westinghouse Electric Corp.
Bloomfield, N.J.

FIXTURES

Jay Lighting Manufacturing Co., Inc.
25 Quincy St.
Brooklyn 38, N.Y.

Lightolier
Jersey City 5, N. J.

Howard Miller Clock Co.
Zeeland, Mich.

Prescolite Manufacturing Corp.
1251 Doolittle Dr.
San Leandro, Calif.

Thomas Industries, Inc.
207 E. Broadway
Louisville 2, Ky.

LOW-VOLTAGE FIXTURES

Loran Fixtures
P. O. Box 911
Redlands, Calif.

WIRING AND CONTROL DEVICES

Arrow-Hart & Hegeman Electric Co.
102 Hawthorne St.
Hartford 6, Conn.

Bulldog Electric Products Co.
7610 Joseph Campau
Detroit 11, Mich.

General Electric Co.
Wiring Device Dept.
95 Hathaway St.
Providence 7, R. I.

Lutron Electronics Co., Inc.
230 Fifth Ave.
Suite 600
New York 10, N.Y.

Minneapolis-Honeywell Regulator Co.
2747 Fourth Ave., South
Minneapolis 8, Minn.

Pyramid Instrument Corp.
Remcon Division
630 Merrick Rd.
Lynbrook, L. I., N.Y.

Square D Electric
Executive Plaza
Park Ridge, Ill.

Superior Electric Co.
Luxtrol Division
83 Laurel
Bristol, Conn.

Thomas Industries
(see above, Fixtures)

Touch-Plate Manufacturing Corp.
Box 1970
Long Beach, Calif.

LUMINOUS CEILINGS

Artcrest Products, Inc.
255 W. 79th St.
Chicago 20, Ill.

Emerson Electric Mfg. Co.
8100 Florissant Ave.
St. Louis 36, Mo.

Luminous Ceilings, Inc.
2500 West North Ave.
Chicago 47, Ill.

Owens-Corning Fiberglas Corp.
Home Building Products Div.
National Bank Bldg.
Toledo 1, Ohio

DIFFUSING MATERIALS, SKYLIGHTS

American Cyanamid Co.
Wasco Division
5 Bay State Rd.
Cambridge 38, Mass.

Filon Plastic Corp.
333 N. Van Ness Ave.
Hawthorne, Calif.

Allied Chemical Corp.
Barrett Division
6510 Bandini Blvd.
Los Angeles, Calif.

Monsanto Chemical Co.
Plastics Division
812 Monsanto Ave.
Springfield 2, Mo.

E. I. du Pont de Nemours & Co., Inc.
Wilmington, Dela.

Rohm & Haas Co.
222 W. Washington Sq.
Philadelphia 5, Pa.

Mississippi Glass Co.
Fullerton, Calif.

GAS LIGHTS

Arkla Air Conditioning Corp.
812 Main St.
Little Rock, Ark.

Bruest, Inc.
Independence, Kans.

Equitable Gas Co.
Pittsburgh 19, Pa.